Adrianne gives us a living memoir, accessible to all. Approached with deep reflection, this book blends personal reflections of identity, faith, relationships, color, and nature in a quest to understand what shapes each of us into who we are and who we are called to be. The utilization of different literary styles adds a deeper texture to the reflections of life. In short, it's an honest and uplifting story of someone striving to love God and people in every way, filled with gratitude, learning, and compassion.

Father Bryan Dolejsi
Archdiocese of Seattle

It was a privilege to listen to God and to Adrianne's life, as I accompanied her for many years as her spiritual director. Adrianne has always been gifted at exploring imagery from her life, the earth, and scripture. These stories reveal the holy work of claiming and integrating different dimensions of her identity, history, and journey across cultures. Adrianne's authenticity and the transforming Spirit of God shine through the illuminated relationships, challenges, changes, and choices. What an inspiring joy to read this memoir, quilting the diverse and beautiful pieces of Adrianne's life, all tied together with sacred, grounded Love.

Sue Fergerson-Johnson
Spiritual Director, Retreat Leader,
Scripture Teacher

If you want to read a memoir that follows a linear chronology, a predictable path of geography, a reliably limited cast of stereotypical characters, and a moral or didactic through line... do not read Adrianne Dyer's personal work My Quilted Memoir. However, if you relish an experience of neck-craning shifts in timelines, a mélange of literary modes, bold transitions of cultural identities and languages, narratives of joy-filled family and encounters of heartbreaking trauma, all braided and woven into a reflective and spiritual textile of the heart, then slowly savor the sights, textures, and art of Adrianne's narrative patches. You will ponder how you can begin with a funeral and end with a boisterously overcrowded family home. You will delight in familial nostalgia and lament for the shared sense of tragedy in the story of Sr. Dianna. You will wonder persistently without answer what single word tethered the ill Santiago to his fleeting reality but still be satisfied that you too have such a word tying you to what is most important in an ephemeral world. Simply linger on the seemingly unrelated patches of various fabrics, threads, and stitches to find an opening where you can connect your own memories, values, and relationships to Adrianne's and then to the universal warp and weft of our common human experience.

Jim Broderick King
Regional Director, Ignatian Spirituality Project

From New Mexico to Japan and in between, Adrianne's reflections beautifully connect her personal story, spirituality, and the natural world. Readers will find a treasure trove of inspiration to help them look deeper at the ordinary in their life and develop an adventurous spirit of discovery.

Sean Doll O'Mahoney, MDiv, BCC
ACPE Certified Educator
Manager, Clinical Pastoral Education

Adrianne's memoir is a rich tapestry of stories honoring her history, culture, and God whose love and grace are woven throughout each quilt square of her life. In the sharing of her joys, sorrows, and desires she invites us to imagine our own life as a quilt, multi-layered and holy. Adrianne's images and prose encourage us to see

Praise for *My Quilted Memoir*

To indwell a book is to dive beyond the words on the page into an experience of living in the story itself. One can easily slip into this book, like putting on an empathetic cloak that allows you to experience an attentive heart that opens your eyes. There is nothing hidden, only an invitation to dance with colors, fabrics, traditions, and life-changing experiences. This memoir becomes an invitation to savor life and step into a nurturing journey.

This book holds an awakening magic as the storytelling mirrors chapters from her journey, creating a quilt assembled with love and challenges. Through Adrianne's voice, you may find your own life flashes before your eyes, with a fluidity that washes away regrets. Each chapter invites a deeper understanding of celebrating our lived spaces to find resonance with the music and faces that surrounds us.

The whole telling of the story invites you to sit as an honored guest at tables of cultural connections. These moments of inclusion and warmth draw you in, making you feel not just like a visitor, but perhaps like part of the family.

Marty Folsom, PhD
Relational Theologian, Executive Director,
Pacific Association for Theological Studies,
Author of *Karl Barth's Church Dogmatics for Everyone* Series
(Zondervan) and *Face-to-Face* Series (Wipf & Stock),
Counseling and Coaching,
Speaker: Theology, Therapy, Bible, Relationships

In this beautifully crafted memoir, the author takes us on a tender journey of vivid memories that are both deeply personal and universally relatable. Themes of love, faith, and self-acceptance weave throughout the colorfully written stories and poems. As a native of New Mexico, the bittersweet essence of nostalgia felt like a warm embrace. It is a heartfelt tribute to the past and a celebration of the resilience found in remembering. A must-read for anyone seeking to reconnect with the familiar echoes of their own story.

Beverly Romero, RN, MSN,
Certified Sound Healer

In *My Quilted Memoir*, you will read the powerful and life-giving spiritual insights of a person who knows the beauty and power of becoming, both individually and in the sacred web of community. In Japan or New Mexico, in a hospital as a chaplain, among her family and friends, Adrianne Dyer shows us what it is to live in the power of the Spirit.

This book explores the author's life as a sacred text. In doing so, she teaches us all how to deepen into the sacred center of our lives. Adrianne asks good questions, such as how am I a gift in this bruised and beautiful world? As she asks such questions, she invites us to reflect on the ways we are a gift in this world. In this way, she is a gifted spiritual director, pointing us to the deeper way. The quilt of our experiences—our joys and sorrows, the mundane and the transcendent—emerge in these pages as a constant invitation.

Reader, enter these pages knowing you are in good hands. You'll come to a place where the Gracious One calls you Beloved. This book invites you to see the world anew. It is a good gift. Rest and explore your spirit in its wisdom and grace.

Reverend Roger Butts
Unitarian Universalist,
Chaplain,
Author of *Seeds of Devotion*

our own story of growth and transformation as a call to heartfelt gratitude for the beauty that life offers us in every moment.

Lisa Dennison
Executive Director of SEEL Puget Sound

My Quilted Memoir is an invitation to holism, story, beautiful wisdom, and community. The word *quilt* is not simply a literary metaphor. Dyer knits her journey for the reader in ways that mend the often-disparate moments and identities of our culture. Our world struggles to hold life together. Dyer's life mosaic is a salve and a meditation for divided souls. Dyer's ancestral wisdom poignantly reveals the depths we can also travel when we are mindful of life's journey.

Rev W. Tali Hairston PhD
Thriving Congregations Seattle Presbytery

Come settle in for a memoir that feels as warm, tender, and personal as its namesake. In *My Quilted Memoir*, Adrianne Dyer weaves together the different textures of essays and poems, memories and reflections, the spiritual and the familial, all together in one poignant package. The resulting collection tells the powerful and emotional narrative of her life so far. Dyer honors beloved ancestors, recounts painful memories, and reflects on her lived experience of racism, all while gently tying each fragment together with her faith. The God Dyer encounters throughout her life is a loving and creative God who feels just as lovely, soft, and enduring as a handmade family quilt.

Rev. Hillary B. Kimsey. Vicar
St. Antony of Egypt Episcopal Church

A natural and engaging storyteller, Adrianne Dyer artistically shares from her loving heart in an enchanting memoir her quintessential quilt comprised of vulnerability, struggle, inner integrity, groundedness in family, integrative faith, God's creativity, gratitude, and extravagant love. While it's often nearly impossible to put down, parts compel pause for reflection. She provokes feelings of elation, frustration, heartbreak, pain by injustice, and also energizes the reader with adventure. Enticingly, she explores her rich Indigenous and Spanish roots and adventurously ascends on her wings to exhilarating heights of transformative self-discovery and self-love. Appealingly, she invites the risk of revealing your authentic self toward intimacy of being known. Unceasingly captivating, she inspires courageous, reflective, and profound journeying, delving more deeply into your roots and venturing on your wings as she creatively empowers the emergence of your quilt—your unique gift to the world.

Rev. Jill Rasmussen-Baker, MDiv, BCC,
ACPE Certified Educator
Director, Spiritual Care

My Quilted Memoir

STORIES
PIECED TOGETHER
from the
FABRIC OF
NEW MEXICO

Adrianne Dyer

Copyright © 2025 by Adrianne Dyer

My Quilted Memoir
Stories Pieced Together from the Fabric of New Mexico

All rights reserved.
No part of this work may be used or reproduced, transmitted, stored, or used in any form or by any means graphic, electronic, or mechanical, including but not limited to photocopying, recording, scanning, digitizing, taping, Web distribution, information networks or information storage and retrieval systems, or in any manner whatsoever without prior written permission from the publisher.
In this world of digital information and rapidly-changing technology, some citations do not provide exact page numbers or credit the original source. We regret any errors, which are a result of the ease with which we consume information.
Without in any way limiting the author's and publisher's exclusive rights under copyright, any use of this publication to train generative artificial intelligence (AI) or Large Language Model (LLM) technologies to generate text is expressly prohibited.

Edited by Laurie Knight
Cover Design by Kristina Edstrom

An Imprint for GracePoint Publishing (www.GracePointPublishing.com)

GracePoint Matrix, LLC
624 S. Cascade Ave, Suite 201
Colorado Springs, CO 80903
www.GracePointMatrix.com
Email: Admin@GracePointMatrix.com

SAN # 991-6032

A Library of Congress Control Number has been requested and is pending.

ISBN: (Paperback): 978-1-961347-86-1
eISBN: 978-1-966346-35-7

Books may be purchased for educational, business, or sales promotional use.
For distribution queries contact Sales@IPGbook.com
For non-retail bulk order requests contact Orders@GracePointPublishing.com

Table of Contents

Foreword 1
Introduction and Invitation 7
Creator God as Artist 13

Part 1
Beautiful Imperfections

Woven in the Aisles of My Life 18
A Beautiful Flower Growing in the Concrete Crack 22
Japanese *Kintsugi* Bowl 27

Part 2
Roots to Wings

A Little Town Off the Old Route 66 32
Community in Community College? 36
Three Most Exciting Sounds in the World 40

Part 3
Being Gift

The Gift of the Sakura Cherry Blossom Tree 46
You Are Gift 49
Yellow and Black Yielding Love to Allow the Both/And 53

Part 4
Remaining Authentic Through Life's Transitions

Dearest Grandma Miquelita 58

Displaced in a Move 62
Cotton Versus Polyester 65

Part 5
Love and Life in a Spanish Song

A Saturday Morning Tradition 70
Celebration of Life and Love 74
Eres Tú, It's You 78

Part 6
Nature's Reflective Wisdom

Earthed 82
A Single Red Leaf 84
A Horse in a Field 86

Part 7
Energy and Life in Playful Shimmer

The Legacy of the Bouncing Knee 90
The Joy and Delight of Physical Activities 93
Beautiful Butterflies 97

Part 8
Essential Truth

Purple Flowers 100
One Word 104
A Different Kind of Emmaus 107

Part 9
To Love and Serve

The Ursuline Sisters' Handprint 112
Love and Serve 116
Love Over Hate, Faith Over Despair 120

Part 10
A Soul Is at Home

Roots from a Little Mountain Town 126

Thousand Square Feet on 138th Street 130
Mi Casita para Mi Alma 134

Conclusion
Assembled and Stitched to Create a Whole 141

About the Author..143

Dedication

For Kale, Jackson, and Isaac. Your steadfast love and unending support are the center of my life, heart, and soul.

With deep love and gratitude for my parents, Joe and Theresa, whose faithful love and commitment to faith, family, and roots are the reasons these stories are lived and embodied in me.

"In curanderismo, the old people teach there is to be no shyness or false modesty about artfulness, for the mother tongue in every person's bloodline, is a sacred poetics."

Dr. Clarissa Pinkola Estés
"The Pope and La Curandera, the Healer"
National Catholic Reporter
August 9, 2010

Foreword

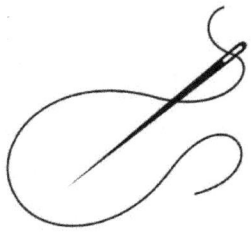

For centuries the majestic Sangre de Cristo Mountains have given life to the peoples of northern New Mexico. The Native Pueblo people, the Spanish, and the contemporary *mestizo* people who inhabit this region today have all been nourished by these sacred and strong mountains. The inhabitants of these communities boast a long and unique interface with each other. Although history has definitely complicated their past, their unique and robust ability to complement one another is remarkable and noteworthy. The manifestations of these profound cultural exchanges are examples of strength and offer a model to the world of how "different" can indeed come together to be remarkable.

The perspectives of the author of this book were born in *los campos de este región* (fields of this region). This area gave her the strength and wisdom to embrace the diverse perspectives, cultures, languages, and spiritualties rooted in the humility of the *mestizo* culture of the Sangre de Cristos. It fed her ability to be strong as she ventured out into the world to stich the quilt that tells the remarkable story of her life. Each stitch and patch bind the story of her journey as she crossed rivers, stumbled over rocks, and made her way through peaks and valleys. As she strives to reach the mountain top, she has uncovered many *cuentos* or stories that tell and shine light on her journey.

This collection of stories is a testament of the author who generously shares and spreads her enduring spirit that was born and fed by the Sangre de Cristos and the people who call this region home. It is a journey of discovery, both for the author and for the reader. Through the lens of personal narrative and historical exploration, the author invites us to delve into the heart of this remarkable region, to understand its past, and to appreciate its enduring legacy. As a *mestiza*, the author embodies the unique blend of Indigenous and Spanish heritage that has shaped this region. This mixed identity has instilled in her a deep sense of resilience, adaptability, and a rich tapestry of traditions. Like the Sangre de Cristos, which have witnessed centuries of change while remaining a constant presence, the *mestizo* people have adapted and thrived, weaving together a vibrant and unique culture.

The author's ability to reveal the challenges and triumphs she has faced in her life's journey have led me to experience emotional and intellectual growth and renaissance in my own identity. The truth is that the intangible realities of tradition, custom, and heritage in one's life are often hard to quantify or even explain. Rather, they are felt as part of one's being. This collection of stories helped me to feel these intangible realities. At several places in the book I found myself smiling, singing, or even hearing the voices of my ancestors. I believe the humble strength and pride of the author is felt as the reader turns every passing page. Reading this collection of short stories became a truly heartfelt experience for me. I am sure you will agree as you read it and make connections to your own traditions, customs, and heritage.

I admire the humble and joyful strength of the author. Her ability to live a life of adventure that took her to new places and peoples is one that I strive to experience myself. I can see how her presence can easily be a blessing to those around her. It is clear that the author's experience in the high desert of New Mexico, in the Pacific Northwest of the United States, in mountains of central Colorado, or of living near the shore in Japan are all experiences felt by the reader. The author has a unique sense of self that is truly a blessing and gift to the reader.

This book offers insights for readers seeking to understand their own heritage and the world around them. I am confident that you will find a rich and rewarding experience that will stay with you long after turning the final page.

Gabriel Antonio Gonzales, EdD

The Dimensional Expressions Found in a Quilt

A quilt, with its diverse uses, is a versatile creation.
It can be functional,
providing warmth and comfort.
It can also serve as a striking decorative feature, enhancing the ambiance of any space,
draping the back of a couch or the surface of a bed.

A quilt can also be created and given to someone as a gift,
handcrafted to mark a special occasion,
like a wedding, a birth, or graduation.
An item to commemorate or weave with a new beginning.

A quilt can also be a storyteller—
a canvas with historical elements woven into the material,
serving as a visual expression of experiences:
joy, sorrow, struggle, strength, courage, and resilience.

Every quilt is a gathering of
pieces of fabric in an array of colors and patterns,
cut into various shapes and sizes.
When assembled and stitched together,
each element creates something beautiful and whole.

The author of a quilt
allows material and fabric to inspire their creativity,
paying attention to how each piece and layer of the quilt
maintains its individual characteristics and utterances.
Fluidly, the author gives license to what the final outcome
longs to be.

Introduction and Invitation

For the last four years, my family and I have had a cross-cultural experience living in Okinawa, Japan. There are many things I can say about Okinawa, specifically that its culture and way of being have broadened my eyes and understanding in new ways. For example, in greeting or being greeted, bowing represents dignity, respect, and gratitude. Despite a language barrier, bowing communicates the worth, value, and honoring of another. There have been days that a simple bow has uplifted my spirits and made me feel noticed and appreciated. Bowing to another acknowledges that we are all interconnected and of significance. This gesture is also woven into Okinawa's concept of being "earthed." The Okinawan people are earthed in their connection and dependence on the land and the sea, their interconnection to family and community, and the handprint and importance of ancestors. This earthed expression has made me think about the land of my family history—the various connections to family, individuals, and communities who have been part of my story and the ongoing handprint of ancestors who continue to shape my perspective and way of being in the world.

I was surprised by how familiar the Okinawa culture was to my roots and culture, a connection I would not have expected to have with a foreign country in the middle of the Pacific Ocean and the South China Sea. Okinawa has a long history of cultural traditions and customs, including the cultivation of crops and gardens along with impressive ingenuity in engineering and construction. The people continually retell their Indigenous and rooted stories through various festivals and rituals. All these facets are woven into their communal way of being. My family roots and history are grounded in a generation of people who lived off the land and grew crops and gardens. Many worked with their hands and bodies in professional vocations and their personal lives. They enjoyed sharing rooted family stories and kept traditions, customs, and celebrations in their communal way of being. This foreign landscape of Okinawa high-lights familiar melodies within me.

While in Okinawa, I read the book *Serafina's Stories* by Rudolfo Anaya. It was an inspirational bridge to my surfacing, reflective thoughts and my cultural roots in New Mexico. *Serafina's Stories,* set in seventeenth century Santa Fe, New Mexico, centers on a group of Pueblo peoples who were suspected of creating a revolution against the government. A dozen Pueblo people were captured and brought before the governor. Among these prisoners is a young woman named Serafina, who is a mestiza, a mix of Spanish and Indigenous. Her character was educated by Spanish Franciscan friars. Therefore, she speaks Spanish fluently. The governor soon discovers that Serafina is a storyteller. This revelation leads to the establishment of a pact between the governor and Serafina. If the governor likes a story she tells, he will release one prisoner. He is captivated by her boldness and intelligence. Serafina's stories provide the governor with the chance to consider and reflect. Her incredible gift for storytelling spares all the prisoners' lives; all are set free.

While Serafina is imprisoned, she is sewing a quilt. This detail grabbed my attention as I started thinking about the many quilts my great-grandma, grandma, and aunts used to make. They used material from slightly worn clothing, leftover fabric from other quilts, and new material to create string tie quilts. These quilts hold an aspect of old and new, remnants of what once was mixed with various fabrics to create a new becoming. There are three components of a string tie quilt: base, patches, and string ties. The base consists of a bottom sheet and batting. Patches of old and new material are sewn together in various shapes and sizes and positioned over the base. Once these layers are carefully placed on each other they are pulled together with string ties. Reflecting on these three elements forged for me the imagery of my life as a literary quilt.

In considering my life as a literary quilt, I recalled all the formative material given to me by my parents, my extended family, and my cultural roots in New Mexico. Many of these experiences and people have remained a foundational "base." I then started to ponder the various places I have lived, my experiences, and the people I have met, professionally and personally. Each represents a colorful "patch" woven into my story. These various experiences and people have all fashioned who I am. The "string ties" within my literary quilt have pulled these layers together and, in doing so, have given rise to a new becoming. The Okinawa culture, *Serafina's Stories,* and the structural nature of a string tie quilt all served as an artistic inspiration to bring aspects of my personal story to the page.

Quilts can tell stories. The material used in quilts can also hold a connection to specific times and places. Sometimes, material in one quilt can be used in another, creating an extended connection between quilts. Yet, what remains true is that a homemade quilt is one of a kind and holds a meaningful connection to the person who created it. As I set out to develop and write my literary quilt, I wanted to use authentic and personal stories. I wanted to highlight a patchwork of experiences and encounters that were significant to me. Like an actual quilt, I used a finite amount of material to create this literary expression. I also wanted this endeavor to serve as a gift, a narrative love letter of gratitude for the meaningful moments and cherished people who have shaped and influenced my life and journey.

As a storyteller, I can relate to the character of Serafina in Rudolfo Anaya's book. Each of the stories Serafina shares has a lesson or insight to offer. I wanted my stories and poems to be invitations for further consideration and not to be answers or applications. Instead, I hope readers allow the stories and poems to highlight joy, sorrow, struggle, resilience, faith, and the journey of transition and transformation. Together, these stories and poems create a beautiful tapestry representing the many handprints in my life.

Each vignette is organically written from the heart. As I stitched these stories and poems together, I noticed that the vignettes sang thematically in sets of three. These groupings share a central theme and hold to the structure of a string tie quilt: base, patch, and string tie. Each collection of stories starts with a rooted tale from my youth, culture, family, etc.—foundational aspects that have remained a cornerstone to who I am (base). The second of the three captures a transcended narrative of various people, places, and experiences I have had (patches). The third speaks to the integration of these grouped stories and how they manifest and metaphorically represent my understanding of self, others, and the Divine. These serve as a bridge to transforming and becoming (string tie).

Thank you for your grace in holding my literary quilt. I hope it will inspire you to consider your personal story as you accompany mine. Ask yourself along the way these questions: What are the experiences and moments that have shaped you? Who are the handprints that have molded or impacted your life? What important aspects of your life have remained foundational? How would your literary quilt serve as a gift, a narrative love letter of gratitude for the meaningful moments and cherished people who have shaped your life and journey? I welcome you to ponder how such reflections transcend or transform your own understanding of self, others, and the Divine, knowing that our lives are beautifully in process.

Creator God as Artist

The courage to step out and write this book started with this reflective story, first published in Abbey of the Arts: Transformative Living Through Contemplative and Expressive Arts, *newsletter Monk in the World Guest Post, January 2024, edited and reprinted with permission.*

God has many names. Often when I look upon nature and my surroundings, I think or find myself saying, "Wow! Look at what God has created." The name of God as creator is true. All around are things that God has created and brought into existence, including myself. Yet God is much more than just a creator. Creator God is also an artist.

So who is this artist God? In contemplating this, I have found that this question has been extended to myself, "Who is the artist within me?" If a creator God, an artistic God created and formed me, then there is also an artist's handprint *within* me. Me, an artist? How can that be? If I can contemplate God being artistic, then I must try to consider this name and expression being true within myself as a created image and likeness, one mirroring the other.

I like to imagine myself sitting across from the artistic God having tea or coffee, getting to know and exploring this artistic layer and depth about God and myself. However, the artistic God doesn't want to only be understood through conversation and dialogue. Instead, the artistic God invites me for a walk. It is in walking that my understanding of artistic God starts to take on a new image and meaning.

While walking with artist God, I am encouraged to slow down, look more closely, and be more attuned to new ways of holding my surroundings. It isn't easy at first. I still want to say to the creator God, "This is beautiful and lovely."

God acknowledges this declaration but gently whispers, "Yes, but can you also see my artistry passionately present in all that I have created?" With love, God says, "Look closer, tell me what you see."

As I look, I find myself noticing details, layers, colors, images, shapes, and depth—hidden expressions. Artistic God stokes this small flame and revelation, constantly encouraging me to utilize all my senses and imagination and to examine and affirm that nothing in creation is one dimensional—not in nature, not in myself.

One day while walking in God's artistic creation, I became curious about a plant I routinely walk by. I do not know this plant's name or species. Each time I have walked past this plant, I have seen it only as a green plant or nondescript bush. Nothing more, nothing less. Yet on this day, I examined this plant for the first time. The leaves have red coloring bleeding into the base of each green one. The red pronounces its relevance and importance, not hidden or separate from the plant, but fully present and integrated—a dimension I had not observed. This plant was more than a living organism. It was also an artistic expression. Metaphorically, this plant was drawing my attention to the artistic expression created within me, a dimension I also have not observed in myself.

God created and formed this plant into existence. It has a purpose and place. Although it is predominantly green, the artistry of God has given this plant a unique detail and expression. As it grows and moves through its season, the crimson tones declare their presence. Red is vibrant, attractive, energetic, mysterious, courageous, and strong. I am lured by the red contribution in this otherwise green plant. This plant is distinctive, whispering a song of surprise and an expression of emergent identity.

While looking upon this plant in its fullness, God's artist voice and created presence engages me with these words:

Querida,

Dear one, you are like this plant—beautifully created from the beginning. With a word, you were breathed into existence, not just with purpose and place, but with passionate love and artistry. You are deeply rooted in your awareness of being created and beloved. However, for too long, you have beheld yourself as simply a green plant. Nothing more, nothing less. Others, including yourself, have walked by and have only seen dynamics and aspects that are easy to perceive. Yet, like the plant, there is more to behold and notice. You are an artistic expression deeply integrated and woven and formed from creative and artistic hands. You are vibrant, warm, inviting, intuitive, ethnic, compassionate, playful, and a wealth of experience and story. Allow the fullness of who you are to emerge and be seen.

Can I dare to see myself as created artistry? Am I purposefully made, and not just another planted soul along the path? I will lean into this invitation and dare to share in the image and likeness given to me as a gift.

Creator and artistic God, thank you for drawing me into a fuller understanding and awareness of who you have made me to be.

Part One

Beautiful

Imperfections

Woven in the Aisles of My Life

I am thankful to have had my maternal grandmother present in my life for fifty years. Though I would not call her grandma, she was known as Nana. Nana and my grandpa were married for over seventy years. Together, they had six children, fourteen grandchildren, and sixteen great-grandchildren. They were each other's best friends and took great delight in one another. Nana's life was both beautiful and imperfect. She could lavish you with enormous love and share wonderful words of affirmation and affection. My Nana could also induce side-splitting laughter with her ability to tell a good story or joke. Unfortunately, she could also deeply wound you with her sassy disposition, fiery opinions, and unabashedly raw comments. Nana was endearing and despite her rough edges she was loved entirely for all that she was. Grievously, in the spring of 2020, my Nana's life came to an end.

Many family members and friends came to Nana's funeral Mass to remember and celebrate her eighty-seven years of life. As the oldest grandchild, I was given the honored role of being able to carry her cremated ashes down the aisle. Standing in the back of the church, awaiting Mass to start, I recalled how my Nana was woven into the aisles of my life. An aisle is like a symbol representing a pathway of life or a spiritual journey. On this day, with her urn in my hands, she and I walked the final aisle of her story together. As I held her urn and ambled down the aisle, I reminisced about all the memories and particularities of who Nana was to me.

I reflected on the deep red wine color of the urn. Red represents vibrance and energy. It also exemplifies deep emotions: anger, love, fire, and joy. Nana was a very passionate person. Red is the perfect color to describe who she was. Nana was full of energy and life. She loved her family fiercely and cherished her friendships. Nana was super social and could make friends in any location. Whether with a grocery store clerk, post office worker, bank teller, etc., she quickly built connections and relationships. She passionately loved all her family and friends, and that passion is what I treasured the most.

I am Nana's first grandchild. When I was very young, she got attached to me and would overindulge me by letting me do whatever I wanted. This dynamic created confusion for me and challenges between my Nana and my parents. Nana wanted to establish who she wanted to be as a grandmother while supporting her adult children as parents. Thankfully, mutual understandings were formed around these various roles and relationships. As a result, there were Nana's house rules and my parent's house rules. Ironically, these house rules were very similar. However, my Nana enjoyed having her home be a place for appropriate freedoms and flexibility to bend the rules. At her heart, my Nana wanted to be a grandma who provided love, joy, affection, sustenance, fun, and laughter to all her grandchildren and great-grandchildren. As a granddaughter, I truly valued her home as a place of reprieve from school and home life. I loved being showered with hospitality, given freedom for self-expression, and being received as myself.

As I continued through the procession, I remembered the years I got to see Nana daily. Every day, from first through eighth grade, I walked to her house after school. When I stepped through the door of her home, she always greeted me affectionately. She tenderly cupped my face, squeezed my cheeks, and kissed me. This greeting was how she welcomed her grandchildren and great-grandchildren, from babies to adults. After such a greeting, she quickly offered me something to eat and told me to relax. My grandparents were not wealthy by any stretch of the imagination, yet they always had food on hand. Nana expressed love through affection and hospitality, notably in her cooking. Whether it was cookies, pies, popcorn, beans, tortillas, her famous New Mexico chili, etc., serving food was one of her love languages. Whether that was an after-school snack or a larger meal around her kitchen table, expressing love with a kiss and food was life-giving to her soul.

I realized I was getting closer to the front of the church. I felt my heart getting heavy. In that tender space, I acknowledged the one aspect of Nana that I would miss the most: her extraordinary ability to tell a story. She loved to share stories and be the keeper of all family narratives. Although she recounted some stories repeatedly, we all loved hearing her tell them. Her ability to bring a story to life was an art. In that moment, I realized I would miss her retelling the story of my being young and wanting her to feed me with a spoon even though I could use the utensil independently. She loved to recall me saying, "Nana, feed me," as I dropped the utensil so she could.

My son especially loved hearing how he became known as "Caffeine Boy." I didn't allow my young son to drink caffeinated soda, but while visiting Nana one summer, she offered him a caffeinated drink. Since it was her house and her rules, she let him have it. This was a treat and a delight for my son, who witnessed Nana's yes to my no. Through this story, they both became endeared to the nickname "Caffeine Boy." At the end of every story, my Nana would always laugh and say, "Oh my golly!" She modeled how to hold stories and memories close and to recall them often.

As I came to the end of the aisle, there was a small table in front of the altar for me to place Nana's urn upon. My heart was flooded with gratitude for all the memories my Nana had given me: gratitude for her faithfulness to her family, her honesty, joy, hospitality, and most of all, her love. My Nana modeled for all of us how to be fully ourselves, even in our imperfections. My mother shared with me that a few days before she died, Nana expressed that I had visited her in her dream. This story brings me to tears, and it also comforts me. I must have been close to my Nana's mind and heart on her final days on this earth. I hope, as her soul slipped away, that she knew how much I loved her and how beloved she was by her whole family.

I slowly placed my Nana's urn on the table. It would be the last time I would be close to her remains. I would no longer feel her hands on my face, hear her laughter, or hear her voice. I realized I was squeezing her (all of her) between my hands. I whispered, "I love you, and thank you." Although this would be the last aisle we would journey together in her story, I would continue to take her handprint, example, and spirit forward into the ongoing pathways of my life.

A Beautiful Flower Growing in the Concrete Crack

While walking, I am often drawn to the wonder of plants and flowers growing in the most obscure places—flowers and plants that thrive in cement cracks, potholes, ditches, against a wall or fence, or even hearty plants growing among sharp lava rocks. I am always in awe of the ones that demonstrate resilience and strength by surviving in the most dubious settings. Vegetation grows and is sustained regardless of the obstacle, barrier, or impediment. Plants such as these remind me of the many underserved and marginalized individuals I would encounter while working as a spiritual care provider at Harborview Medical Center in downtown Seattle, WA —resilient, strong, and courageous individuals who have navigated insurmountable challenges and barriers in their lives.

I completed my Clinical Pastoral Training (CPE) at Harborview Medical Center, a level one adult and pediatric trauma center, to become a medical spiritual care provider/chaplain. Harborview is also the primary medical safety net for the local region, serving and caring for the urban underserved. In this medical setting, I engaged in various human stories, including with those who were the most vulnerable. Each patient I encountered changed my perspective and heart—not out of pity but out of awe for how they faced numerous challenges and struggles. Fr. Greg Boyle, founder of Homeboy

Industries (the world's most extensive gang rehabilitation and re-entry program), often says that we need to be people and communities of compassion. The type of compassion that can stand in awe at what the poor must carry, rather than standing in judgment of *how* they carry it. This is the kind of compassion where one is willing to put oneself in another person's shoes and be changed. One patient, Matthew, helped me stand in awe of the beautiful and fragile components that can conspire to impact one's life. In this encounter, I also gained a broader language of acceptance and love.

Matthew was admitted to Harborview for multiple organ failure. He had an extensive substance use history and was undergoing treatment for substantial health failures. Sadly, his overall condition was in decline. Matthew grew up Catholic and wanted to reconnect to his faith as a source of strength and comfort during his hospital stay. I was invited to come and provide emotional and spiritual care support. He was understandably uncomfortable, tired, irritable, and easily agitated. He was often tearful, angry, tender, and sometimes mean. I never knew what kind of mood he would be in when I visited. After navigating his initially guarded disposition, he eventually regarded me as a trusted and supportive companion.

Matthew considered my visits a safe space. He often shared aspects of his personal story with me. He revealed the catalyst events that impacted his substance use. Regrettably, it created an estrangement between himself and his family and friends and included a time when he was without stable housing and no community. Matthew shared that, at times, he did his best to simply survive. He often spoke of shame and guilt for the decisions he made. He also expressed regret for how his substance use impacted his loved ones, his ability to sustain employment, and the eventual negative impact on his body. Matthew noted that shame, guilt, and anger had hardened his view toward life, God, self, and others. His bitterness and pessimistic outlook kept him stuck in desperate survival patterns and isolated places.

As I listened to Matthew share, I thought of the solo plants I have often seen growing along a cement wall or in cracks and crevices. Drawing attention to say, "I'm here, alive, but alone." Like these plants, Matthew was overlooked and sometimes pulled or removed from one seemingly secure location to be placed in another. Each time, he had to replant somewhere new. Matthew had to carry his internal wounds and struggle to each new place of replanting, often feeling isolated and alone. All while trying to remain engaged and present to life around him.

Matthew shared that he longed to make amends with his mother. We contacted his mother and asked her to come to the hospital. She came and continued to visit with him during his hospital stay. She demonstrated compassion and grace in each visit. Her presence appeared to be of comfort and healing for them both. I witnessed a softening coming over Matthew, and his anxiety soon lessened. Unfortunately, his medical condition continued to worsen. Over time, he faced end-of-life care.

Understandably, this was distressing physically, emotionally, and spiritually for Matthew. Regardless of the support system a patient has in making these decisions, it is a scary and an isolating place to be. Whatever happens, the patient is the one who will experience the outcome. Matthew came to an acceptance that end-of-life care was his next step. In that transition, death would most likely come swiftly. During this tender time, Matthew leaned on the support of his mother, the medical staff, and me. The courage and resilience he once relied on to fight through life's challenges to survive were then the reservoirs of strength he came to draw upon as he faced the end of his life.

Matthew asked to see a priest to receive the Sacrament of Reconciliation for forgiveness and healing. Initially, he found comfort in the priest's visit. Yet doubt crept in as to whether his verbal confession was sufficient for his soul to be allowed into heaven. He wanted to know what I thought. With humility, I could not commit to a definitive answer as to what life after death fully entailed. However, I did name my belief in God's covenant love for all humanity: a love that is never ending. I shared that God's love draws near to us always, even in our final days on this earth. I provided a simple question to address Matthew's fear and anxiety. I said, "The God of love asks each of us one question, 'Do you love me?'"

I shared with Matthew the gospel story of Jesus visiting Peter on the beach after Jesus's resurrection. In the story, Peter feels deep remorse, shame, and guilt for denying his friendship with Jesus, a denial he committed three times. His deep regret and anguish were distressing. I helped Matthew understand that the feelings Peter experienced were the same for him. Tearfully, he made the connection. I continued sharing that in the story, Jesus asks one question of Peter. One question he repeats three times. "Peter, do you love me?" Then I looked at Matthew and said, "Jesus has one question for you. 'Matthew, do you love me?'" He began to cry.

Matthew and I spent time discussing his image and understanding of love, naming all the ways he had experienced love throughout *his* story. Together, we recalled when love was shared, given, and received. He also expressed the times when love was denied, blocked, or absent. Each recounted story of love served as a bridge to understanding God's love in Jesus's question, "Do you love me?" In reflection, Matthew would answer that question for himself three times. It was a tender and holy moment to witness and absorb. Tears flowed from my eyes and his. It was the first time I saw peace in Matthew's brow and overall disposition. Love showered over both of us in this truly sacred moment.

We lingered in this space as Matthew and I shared tears of release, joy, and laughter. His spirit was no longer heavy. Like a beautiful flower growing in the cracks of the cement, Matthew was showing life and vigor, but this time saying, "I'm here, alive, and not alone." I sensed he understood deep inside that he was not just forgiven but dearly loved. Witnessing love and life in that moment is something I will never forget. Grievously, three days later, Matthew died.

It would have been easy to focus only on the loss at the end of Matthew's life and how he navigated cracks, crevices, rocks, and difficulties. Indeed, his story is one of struggle, loss, and hardship. Yet it is also one of beauty, triumph, resilience, and celebration. Like a flower proclaiming its life in the most obscure place, Matthew represents humanity's duality. We are all beautiful imperfections, each poking through our various settings, whether that is from the cracks or within lush garden beds, souls announcing from deep within, "I am here, I am alive, longing to be seen, understood, and known."

Japanese Kintsugi Bowl: My Self Portrait

Kintsugi is a Japanese art that restores broken pottery. Cracks are mended, and broken pieces from a pottery bowl are put back together with golden glue. Metaphorically, a kintsugi bowl is a visual reminder to find beauty in life's imperfections. The golden glue illuminates cracks and flaws versus hiding them away. Broken aspects of a human narrative are real. A kintsugi bowl celebrates all facets of life by giving awe to, and highlighting, the resolve and resilience within cracks and flaws, honoring and celebrating humanity entirely. It is not an either/or expression but a beautiful portrait of the both/and.

My Kintsugi Bowl

Childhood is filled with love and struggle.
You know you are a gift and delight to your parents and
loved ones.
But while navigating growth, challenges,
pressure, worry, and expectations,
cracks intentionally or unintentionally occur.

It takes a village to raise a child, a common phrase of wisdom.
Extended family, neighbors, teachers, friends, and community members

hold power individually or collectively.
All influencing and impacting a child positively or negatively, and yet,
cracks, intentionally or unintentionally, can occur.

Moving is a season of transition and change.
A disorienting time of acclimating and familiarizing with something new.
Opportunities and experiences provide new learning and growth.
Yet, measurables and success can be translated differently.
A broken piece of the bowl falls away.

Being employed and providing for oneself is a liberating and bumpy road,
a schedule full of work, friendships, family, bills, and other pursuits.
Youthful energy keeps the juggling act going forward,
yet, more is needed to attend to what is growing under the surface:
Cracks intentionally or unintentionally occur.

Two souls in friendship and love set out to build a family
and a home.
Two hearts are eager to set roots and cultivate a village for others and their own.
That journey will welcome "a blessing" and "a gift," two treasures dearly beloved,
while also holding the memory of two souls lost, equally wanted and loved.
A broken piece of the bowl falls away.

In life's natural progression, a family of four will undergo a transition.
The oldest will leave and no longer reside at home as before.
Three members will proceed to a new country, while the eldest pledges to serve his own.
In this new location, a pronounced silence and contemplation are formed.

The golden glue of love and grace draws the soul's attention to cracks and broken pieces.

Saints and ancestors come and attend to the soul,
listening and addressing wounds received in the lived narrative,
acknowledging hurts with compassion and kindness while
speaking of goodness, no matter the flaws created.
Grace and love mixed in gold fill intentional and unintentional cracks that have been formed.

Profound fatigue surfaces from deep within.
The years of striving to meet measurable expectations and goals:
successes, setbacks, opportunities, and losses.
Seeking to find affirmation and importance.
*Grace and love mixed in gold mend broken pieces,
claiming one's genuine place of being known.*

The Holy Spirit is an advocate, counselor, and guide.
Gently nudges and discloses the mirror of the heart.
It reveals the various forms of fear and protection:
Places that are divided, hidden, and sectioned into pieces.
Grace and love mixed in gold glue, broken pieces, restoring the soul into wholeness.

A soul's inner bowl has experienced many unfoldings,
undergoing cracks and broken and severed pieces.
Yet restoration and mending reveal a transformation.
Grace and love illuminate the entire human essence.
A soul accepts, embraces, and honors all elements of life as part of the whole.

Part Two

Roots to Wings

A Little Town Off the Old Route 66

Grants is the name of the town I was born and raised in—located off the old Route 66 in New Mexico. Grants is a small, high desert town, seventy miles west of Albuquerque and is considered the entrance to national parks and Indigenous pueblos. The Zuni Mountains lie to the west with Mount Taylor (a volcano) and the San Mateo Mountains to the north. The region around Grants also has mesas, lakes, and rugged lava rock formations. Historically, farming, railroads, and mining were all part of its economy. Although this is my town of origin, it represents much more than just a location on a map. I have come to realize that where I am from is a place that has shared hopes, equity among the people in the community, mutual respect for a job well done, and individual investment in the overall experience of this place. My memories from Grants include those with family, friends, neighbors, and everyday experiences. These memories hold joy and some sadness. My hometown is imprinted on my life and story.

Those who lived in Grants were connected to the uranium mining industry. This mining industry was the primary economic engine for the town. There were many opportunities for people to find work at the mine or in the connected supporting industries. These jobs required physical labor, a specific skill set, or managerial leadership.

If people were willing to work hard, they could find a job. These opportunities were not seen as a trapped existence but rather an avenue to make a meaningful and fulfilling life. So much so that many people graduated from the local high school, married someone from the town, and settled within the community. Most people were able to afford a home and raise a family. Not everyone stayed in Grants, and most who ventured off returned to visit family and friends who had remained.

One dynamic that added to the equity of the Grants experience was that neighborhoods and homes were similar in square footage and value. As a young girl, I remember riding my bike and playing with my neighborhood friends, all of whom had homes similar to mine. As we rode our banana-seat bikes through the streets, we saw that one neighborhood mirrored the next. I didn't realize this until later, but this allowed for significant comfort and familiarity as I circled the streets near my own. In addition, stores, shops, and restaurants reflected the community's income. I shopped, dined, attended church, and participated in similar activities with my peers. We all went to the same movie theater, swam at the same public pool, and ate at the pizza restaurant in town. We even experienced the same one-hour trip to visit the big city of Albuquerque. A similar lifestyle built a shared connection among those who lived in and called Grants home.

The mines brought people of various stories and backgrounds to live and work in Grants. Half of the population was Hispanic or Latino, while the other half was made up of different ethnic groups such as Native Americans, African Americans, Asians, Filipinos, Caucasians, and Europeans. My neighbor George was an immigrant from Austria. He initially immigrated to Canada and then to New Mexico to work in the mines. Like my father, he was a hard worker with a strong work ethic. They were similar in that each desired to own their own home and to provide for their families.

This familiar story wove the community together and created a foundation that, although unspoken, was known to all.

Common routines were also shared experiences. Saturday mornings were occupied by helping my dad with yard work. My assistance would include raking, weeding, sweeping, and watering the grass edges. It was not uncommon for my dad and our neighbors to all be mowing their yards at the same time. Often, this would culminate when engines would stop, and a cluster of neighbors gathered to chat, and inevitably, to share some beers. From a distance, I saw laughter, watched them pointing at their yards, and I could only imagine the stories they were telling and the triumphs they were celebrating. Their ability to work, provide for their families, and have mutual connections gave them a sense of contentment and satisfaction. Though my neighbors and I came from different backgrounds and stories, the common language of working hard and supporting those in the community was foundational.

In addition to having good neighbors and friends, we also had many family members who lived in Grants. Having aunts, uncles, and other cousins close to my age created natural playmates with whom I had several shared experiences. Easter egg hunts in the mountains, camping, fishing, riding bikes, sleepovers with the grandparents, holidays, or visiting one another on the weekend were common. I also enjoyed having my godparents, *Nino and Nina*, nearby. They each bestowed kindness and affection upon me. My *Nina* showered me with handmade gifts, and I always had an open reservation in her hairdresser chair.

I benefitted by seeing my grandparents every day after school, having an aunt to play with, and having an uncle to drive me to the local Sonic for an after-school slushy or chili cheese hot dog. It was also fun to go with my grandpa to see my uncle play high school basketball. My grandpa would give me a few dollars and allow me to roam throughout the gymnasium. My fifteen years living in Grants was the only time in my life that I would live in such close proximity to my family, experiencing aspects of life together, going to school, working, and being community. A familiar routine we could relate and share in.

Like many mining communities, my hometown also shared a common vulnerability. When uranium was no longer economically viable, the mines in Grants shut down. The revenue and employment generated in Grants were only sustainable with the mining industry. Businesses and other professions soon left to find more profitable locations. The result was that many people moved away to find work elsewhere, my family included. This growing and vibrant town slowly faded away.

The town of Grants still remains nestled off Route 66. Yet, the place I grew up in has long since disappeared. The seeds of hope, equity, respect, and shared contribution were rooted deeply. Remarkably, some of these same themes have remained with the people who have continued to live in Grants despite the deteriorated setting, homes, shops, and vacant buildings. It continues to be a gateway for national parks, Indigenous pueblos, and it holds historical museums of the handprints that were part of shaping this small, high desert town. The inspiring resiliency of those who have stayed in Grants continue to hold on to the good, see the beauty in the surroundings, and are a supportive and welcoming community. Their spirits are like a steadfast thread, stitching a town and community together with the beauty that remains even among the remnants of what once was.

Community in Community College?

Leaving my roots in New Mexico was complex. Being so far from family, culture, and a rooted place of belonging was hard. Yet, leaving also expanded my horizons and awakened me to new opportunities, experiences, and relationships. The tension between roots and wings would follow me through many life transitions, weighing the importance of maintaining my roots and discovering the hidden longings and gifts deep within my soul. Figuring out how to hold roots and wings simultaneously would become a journey in every life threshold I would cross. The first of those thresholds would be graduating from high school and considering higher education.

Both of my parents went to trade schools for their specific professions. Although my mother eventually received her BA in education as an adult, I would be the first in my family to go from high school to college—a journey that was unfamiliar to me and equally to my parents. We navigated and sometimes disagreed on how best to start that journey. Luckily, my parents knew I wasn't ready to go from high school to a four-year university. I didn't know what I wanted to study, so community college became an encouraged first step, and one that was right for me.

Upon graduation, many high school students consider attending a four-year university. Rarely is community college their first wish. It can be perceived as being on the junior varsity rather than on the varsity team. Often students who attend community college want to get in and get out as soon as possible. There is no need to establish or root in such a temporal location. Hence, finding community within a community college can be challenging. Thankfully, my journey in community college would not follow that pattern. Instead, I established significant friendships, had the opportunity to serve in student government, and learned how to embrace, articulate, and understand what it means to be a minority.

Academically, community college provided smaller classes that allowed for more interaction with professors for instructional support. I came to believe that my professors took a vested interest in my success as a student and as a young person. For example, I had exited high school with little confidence in my ability as a math student. One professor infused in me a newly found lens that allowed me to see my potential in a different light. This created a transformation in thought that would lay a foundation for my willingness to risk and believe in myself and my potential.

Smaller classes also created the opportunity to engage with peers. This dynamic led to my making significant friendships with likeminded individuals. It was refreshing to find others also discerning the questions of life, love, school, career, family, and faith. I often spent time with my friends after classes, on the weekends, at school events, and enjoying one another's company. We played, laughed, and teased one another often to avoid taking the liminal space we were experiencing so seriously. When deeper conversations transpired, we genuinely supported each other without judgment. We encouraged each other to listen to the goals and desires in our hearts as we navigated the tension of holding roots to wings. These friends left and attended different universities, found careers, and created new friendships. Yet, the memories and special bonds formed left a long-lasting impression. I have seen each of us become more than who we were in community college.

Some of these friendships were formed and cultivated while participating in student government. Serving as a member of the student government created opportunities to support the student body and the college's mission and vision. In my first year, I campaigned to be a freshman representative. This was my first time campaigning to hold a leadership role in anything. Incredibly, my opponent and I tied for the position on election day. At that moment, I confessed that I had not voted for myself. In fact, I didn't cast a vote at all. Not out of a lack of self-confidence, but I didn't want to appear arrogant. My friends enjoyed teasing me about my naive mistake. Thankfully, I won the revote and learned from the experience. I became the freshman representative and earned the role of secretary the following year. Both times, I made sure I cast a vote. Student government became the seed that would germinate my belief that I could have an impact on others and my community.

During my second year of community college, I was approached and invited by a school administrative staff member to speak at a leadership luncheon where I would share my experience as a community college student. I felt honored to be asked to participate in such an event. Little did I know that the intent of this luncheon was to create a narrative that our school was dynamically supporting minority students. I was not told this was the focus of the luncheon until I arrived. To this day, I cannot accurately recall what I may have talked about. Yet, I remember feeling blindsided and used as a character to support someone else's objective.

This experience enlightened my awareness of the differences in perspectives and assumptions of how people view minorities. Minorities share many commonalities. However, each person's narrative is unique. At this event, I was not asked to tell my story as a minority. I was asked to tell the story of a student attending their college, who happened to be a minority. The integrated reality of my story and my current experience was not being embraced. I realized then, that my minority account was not equally valued or understood. Although this experience was not a class I was enrolled in, it was formative and impacted my awareness. Without hearing or embracing each person's narrative, minorities end up becoming a singular group.

My two years in community college produced memories I still smile upon. It was a journey in finding my strengths, providing a solid space of safety to stumble, and find success along the way. I discovered academic achievement and formed long-lasting friendships. Attending community college created an opportunity for me to serve others through student government, which only strengthened my confidence and heart to be of impact to those around me. Though it did not feel glamorous to tell others that I was going to community college after graduation, it ended up being the perfect setting. It created the space for me to listen to the hopes and dreams within me, assisted in shaping and claiming my voice as a person of color, and enabled me to develop skills to navigate the ongoing journey of holding to both roots and wings.

Three Most Exciting Sounds in the World (It's a Wonderful Life)

Every Christmas Eve, we watch *It's a Wonderful Life.* Watching this movie has not only become a tradition, but like most things that become cyclical, I can't help but gain more profound wisdom and insight each time I watch it. This poem is for George Bailey—perhaps even for myself. It speaks to the tension of holding to family, to roots, and listening and stepping into the melody of the soul that also calls us forward, beyond.

> *George Bailey asks Uncle Billy, "Do you know the three most exciting sounds in the world?" Uncle Billy says, "Sure. Breakfast is served. Lunch is served. Dinner is served."*
>
> *George responds, "No, Anchor chains, plane motors, and train whistles."*

Words of Wisdom for George Bailey
(including myself)

George Bailey, you are fun, engaging, and wise.
You love your family, friends, and community.
You are constantly devoted to the people who have shaped your story and journey.

Since you were a child, you have always wanted to see and experience
settings beyond your home of Bedford Falls.
The sounds of exploration, architecture, and adventure abide,
deep in the background of your heart's longing.

"Anchor chains, plane motors, and train whistles."
Your subscription to *National Geographic* has only
fostered and cultivated this hunger and longing
to grow, expand, and risk your place of knowing.

However, each time, doors of opportunity came for you to risk and step out,
unforeseeable circumstances also entered,
redirecting your heart and listening.
Your response each time was to be loyal, dutiful, and responsible.

You never want to hinder or burden those you love.
You choose the sounds of breakfast, lunch, and dinner to stabilize those around you.
You are a noble man who sacrifices for others,
keeping your longings remote and distant in the background.

You are sure that your deep desires could never be a reality.
Never once have you considered that your deep longings
are just as crucial as providing sustainability and care to others.
The aspect of *either/or* is prevalent to all you know.

Holding your longings and others' needs doesn't have to be an *either/or*.

Each day, each season of life is much more about an aspect of *both/and.*
There could be a balanced tension to care for yourself and those you love.

Could you imagine that stability and adventure can both be present?
Both are essential to being whole.
Or has stability become a sense of safety and protection? Comfort and control?

George Bailey, it is vital to listen to your deepest longings.
Pay attention to the sounds of your heart.
Anchor chains, plane motors, and train whistles.

What are these sounds saying to you? Can you trust they are essential to listen to?
Can you see expressions of these sounds in your life?
What would it look like to cultivate and risk being in these longings more?

Stability and adventure are part of the balance of life.
Life draws change, transition, and even transformation in us all.
Movement and growth are constantly present; life, in its essence, is not stagnant.

George, it's time to listen and keep the sounds in your life balanced and
find peace in the routine of breakfast, lunch, and dinner
while also finding ways to express your deepest longings, which may play a different melody.

"Every time a bell rings, an angel gets its wings," says your young daughter.
Wings represent wholeness, balance, and freedom.
Can you hear the bells in your spirit inviting you to wholeness, balance, and freedom?

Life, indeed, is wonderful!
Listen to the melody and the sounds deep within your soul.
Open yourself to respond to the integrity created within you.

Part Three

Being Gift

The Gift of the Sakura Cherry Blossom Tree: A Tribute to My Tia Orcelia

In Japanese, sakura means cherry blossoms. Sakura trees are a variety of cherry trees that grow in Japan but do not produce fruit. Instead, these trees bloom each spring with beautiful pink and white flowers in various sizes and structures. In their flowering season, they draw attention to the places they grow. Their soft blossoms have a sweet fragrance that perfume the air, yet their flowering season will only last a few weeks. Within that time, people celebrate, gather, walk among the blooming trees, hold festivities, and embrace the gift and symbolism of the sakura cherry tree.

Our human journey on this earth is limited and will fade away. The sakura's short blossom season is a reminder that life is to be savored, embraced, and not taken for granted. Getting attached to material things, status, wealth, etc., can only interfere with or prohibit embracing life to the fullest. Bitterness, anger, regret, and shame are emotions that can withhold seeing life in its moments of goodness and richness. Festivals during the sakura blossom season represent the importance of spending time with loved ones and cherishing their lives. The sakura illuminates the importance of joy, hope, renewal, appreciation, and the gift of life in nature and one another.

As I have contemplated the meaning of the sakura cherry blossom tree, it has formed a deeper reflection. The sakura tree reminds me of a beloved tia. My Tia Orcelia embodied the beauty and meaning of the sakura tree. This poem is in remembrance of her.

In the early budding phase of the sakura tree,
my heart remembers your warm hug and welcoming spirit.

As the blossoms on the tree start to break forth,
I remember your affectionate smile and the sparkle of love in your eyes.

As the flowers come into fullness, a sweet scent perfumes the air.
I remember the intoxicating fragrance of your joyful spirit and laughter.

The birds perch themselves among the supportive branches, and
I remember your grounded faith that helped you navigate good, complex, and challenging times.

As the sunlight illuminates the beauty of the delegate petals,
I remember your sincere ability to see the good and positive in others and circumstances.

Festivals and family gatherings mark the sakura cherry season.
I remember your love of family gatherings, celebrating, and singing together.

As the petals start to cross over, their fragrance slowly fades.
I am reminded of the swift diagnosis that drew your fatality near.

The sakura blossoms conclude.
I recall drinking in every detail of my last visit with you,
marveled by your extraordinary peace, courage, and acceptance deep within.
Your beautiful soul left this earth, leaving both impact and memory.

In remembrance of you,
I want to carry the essence of the sakura cherry tree embodied in you:
to look for the goodness and positivity in life and others.

In remembrance of you,
I want to be a blooming tree to lift another person's soul, and
to celebrate and walk in their joys, wounds, successes, and sorrows.

In remembrance of you,
I want to laugh often, no matter what unfolds, and
to personify characteristics of mercy, love, and grace.

In remembrance of you,
I want to be open, generous, and hospitable to others,
to offer my whole self just as you did for me and those around you.

In remembrance of you,
I desire to have grounded faith and embrace the gift of life,
to be grateful in all things, acknowledging that life will fade away.

In remembrance of you,
I hear your whispering voice among the blossoming sakura cherry trees:
Live life with great faith, hope, joy, and love.
Embrace life and those around you, cherish times together.
Welcome and seize each moment and day as a gift.

You Are Gift

Sometimes, a song, poem, photograph, or even a movie can illuminate something stirring under the surface. The Disney movie *Encanto* was that movie for me. There were features within the characters of the movie that I could relate to. The story centers around the Madrigal family. The characters Alma (the abuela, grandma) and Mirabel (granddaughter) embodied elements similar to my own story. Throughout the movie, these characters go through a pivotal moment of collapse and move into a new place of self-discovery. Alma and Mirabel echo similar characteristics to my lived journey of fear, protection, yearning, releasing, and claiming who I am as a gift.

Alma's story is a tale of grief and loss. Due to conflict and unrest, she is forced to flee from her family of origin, roots, and culture. She is alone with three small children. She leans toward fear and protection as survival tools to aid her new beginning. In that unfolding, she relies heavily on each of her family members having a gift to contribute to the community. In Alma's thinking, having a gift gives them purpose, a role, and a way to contribute. If you are of value, then you are protected and safe.

I can relate to Alma's story. When I moved away from my culture and family of origin in New Mexico, I was unsure what it meant to belong somewhere new. In New Mexico, if you were Hispanic, you would be seen as a person of culture and someone with gifts and talents to contribute to the whole. You could live in your talents independently of your culture. If you succeeded within your gifts, your culture was not separated. I know this thought was not always equally held by everyone, nor was this freedom equally experienced generationally. However, growing up, I never felt like I had to choose between those dynamics within me. I could be a person of culture and live within my gifts and talents.

However, when I moved away, the confidence to live in the fullness of myself didn't feel safe. Like Alma, I found comfort in fear and protection. Though no one communicated to me directly that I must choose between my gifts and culture, I had an awareness that I needed to pick one and minimize the other. On the positive side, fear and protection contributed to my ability to be consistent, dependable, and hard working. Not wanting to disappoint others drove me to become an excellent team member, willing to take on new challenges.

On the surface, the fruits of these attributes appeared excellent and beneficial. I even received affirmation, validation, and recognition for achievements. However, fear and self-protection were consistently present in my inward dialogue. Those voices said, "If I work hard enough, contribute, and be of value, then surely I will belong. If I belong, I will not be alone, and hopefully, I won't be afraid; I will be safe."

The world is often conditional, and to place such tender hope in the capacities of inherently flawed institutions and equally wounded people only reinforced my tendency for fear and self-protection. Eventually, the foundations of my interior self-belief started to crumble.

Within this fragile and fragmented space, a new voice started to emerge. Like Mirabel, a voice within me sang forth, asking, "What is my gift, and who am I as a gift?" Mirabel is a character in search of a gift. Since she was not given a specific role or talent, she was not as woven into the family as those given particular gifts. She was not less important but was without an outward expression to be of value. My survival habits only created division within me. I desired to be my authentic self, whole and complete. I did not want to be divided within myself anymore. I desired to be accessible and express my most authentic self, and I wanted to be free from the expectation of either/or intentionally or unintentionally placed upon me. This divided reality could no longer sustain my interior soul, and the protective elements started to shatter. In this internal rubble, Our Lady of Guadalupe came and visited me.

Our Lady of Guadalupe is a beautiful image of the both/and. She, like me, is both Indigenous and Spanish. She represents the bridge between nations, conveying that they (we) are also one. In her fullness, she gently sang these words to me:

> *La tierra ha dado origen a vuestra cultura y fe,*
> *The land has given rise to your culture and faith.*
> *You no longer need to choose between the various aspects of yourself.*
> *You can hold your culture and all that has unfolded in your story.*
> *You can share from the intellect and also from your authentic heart.*
> *You can speak English and express yourself in Spanish.*
> *Eres maravillosamente hispana,*
> *You are wonderfully Hispanic.*
> *You can bring your gifts to those you meet every day,*
> *and to an assigned job or specific role.*
> *Security at times is needed*
> *without allowing fear and protection to entomb you.*
> *No tengas miedo,*
> *Don't be afraid.*
> *Your past is just as important as the present and future.*
> *Embrace the "both/and" within you*
> *embodying rich, rooted soil and new experiences.*

You no longer need to choose whom to be.
Be a person who is, in fact, a living whole gift of
"both/and,"
ser Guadalupana, be Guadalupana.

At the end of the *Encanto* story, Alma, Mirabel, and the Madrigal family watch the collapse of their home. Through that broken place, they experience healing and restoration. Alma understands she can no longer maintain a posture of fear and protection. It is time to release that survival mindset. I, too, experienced the same release in the healing words of Our Lady of Guadalupe. Her words, sung to me, also paralleled the end of *Encanto*. Mirabel's family sings, revealing truths about who she is as a gift. Mirabel responds, "I can see all of me." The beautiful words given to me by Our Lady of Guadalupe have allowed me to start to see all of me. I am rooted, gifted, cultured, an embodied essence of both/and. I am a gift.

Yellow and Black
Yielding Love to Allow the Both/And

What is your favorite color?
What color best describes you?
Such a question often draws a blank.
What color fits these questions?

Deep down, the color of these questions is yellow.
Happiness, optimism, energy, and active imagination.
Joyful, creative, and enthusiastic.
Yet, somehow, black is also present in my dominant attire, thinking, and attachment.

Black is unique, mysterious, and intelligent.
Versatile, strong, practical, and grounding.
Intriguing, robust, formal, and seductive.
It also embodies grief, mourning, darkness, and sadness.

So which is it? Which color, yellow or black, defines me?
By maintaining both, do they enhance or hinder the other?
Yellow is bold and draws attention.
Black is an edged detail, a shadow, and relatively inconspicuous.

Yet both are present within me, sometimes creating tension and collision.
Yellow naturally brings joy, hope, laughter, and happiness.
Black, in partnership with spontaneous yellow
offers pop, clarity, and beautiful definition.

This blend of yellow and black can be a positive energy that draws others in.
Yet, black whispers in the shadows, "This is not good; time to hide, tone this boldness down."
Yellow soon cowers, and the color black becomes the more pronounced hue.
Leaving yellow to feel betrayed and deceived by black's language of fear and pessimism.

It would seem that both yellow and black could get along and find some kind of balance.
Both provide comfort, a sense of belonging, and purpose.
Yet when they share equal roles, they end up morphing into expressions of
caution, hazard, danger, and heightened fear of obstruction.

So how do these colors, one created and the other formed, coincide?
Both want some way to exist and flourish.
One color was created initially and desires to be accessible to reveal itself naturally.
The other color feels relevant due to the formed information, direction, and thoughts constructed.

Yellow knows it is better with black's mysterious detail, uniqueness, and intrigue
while black also knows it needs yellow as an accent in the process of being more revealing.
Yellow becomes more radiant when it is free to be the dominant hue.
With black as a striking contrast, it adds to yellow's sophistication and power.

What will be the culmination of these two colors? Will this tension continue?
In love, black yields, deciding it's best to complement and support yellow's vitality,
choosing to allow yellow to be the fully manifested color.
With delight, black witnesses yellow becoming more vibrant each day in the now and forever after.

Part Four

Remaining Authentic Through Life's Transitions

Dearest Grandma Miquelita,

With love and gratitude, I write this letter to you. I always remember you. Your children, grandchildren, and great-grandchildren continue to speak of your kindness, generosity, and tender heart. Attributes shared about you often bring a glistening of tears over their eyes. You are never forgotten. I am thankful for your example of love, courage, and deep faith. Stories shared about you have impacted the next generation of your descendants. We are all better people because of you.

Grandma, when I was young, I enjoyed observing your physical nuances and the way you moved through your day. In delight, I watched you brush your silver hair, make a small braid, and form it into a small bun. Your petite, sun-kissed hands were delicate but strong—hands that served as your tools and instruments in your life. You wore a simple gold wedding band on your finger, a sign of devotion to my grandpa. Your clothes were simple, tidy, and practical, which allowed you to bend and move around your home and land. Over your clothes you wore a simple handmade wrap-around apron as part of your everyday routine. Grandma, this apron embodied the essence of who you were. A woman who understood that life could be messy, your apron was an expression of hospitality and service, and a garment that was as routine as your prayer and faith.

You wore this cotton apron every day to protect your clothing. Cotton is a material that is absorbable but also breathable; therefore, messy elements could still penetrate through. Grandma, at a young age you experienced how swiftly life can change. Your mother and one of your sisters died from the flu, during the 1918 epidemic. Tragically, you were over the mountains visiting extended family when this occurred. Due to travel and risk of infection you stayed with your extended family and did not return home. At twelve years old, you became displaced from your family. You often said, "We are all here on borrowed time." You understood that in a moment, an illness, injury, or death could alter life. You imparted wisdom to your family to never take life or those around them for granted. You understood that life could change unexpectedly and become messy.

Grandma, sadly your life consisted of many tragedies, complexities, and challenging elements. You lived through the struggles of the depression, moved away from your roots to follow my grandpa for work, experienced the death of an infant, and before you left this earth you mourned the death of your parents, husband, siblings, some of your adult children, and a few grandchildren. Yet, despite these dynamics, you never became bitter, hard, or guarded. Your spirit remained organically cotton: receivable, grounded, earthed.

Grandma, your tender heart longed to protect your loved ones from struggle, change, and heartache, yet you understood these aspects of life were unavoidable. You demonstrated how to remain open to life without becoming hardened. You often said, "We need to accept all that God gives us." You trusted that God would never purposely create or put challenges upon us. Instead, you reminded us to posture ourselves to accept and receive the negative and positive elements of life equally, embracing goodness, joy, sorrow, hardship, the bitter, and the sweet with the same amount of grace and allowing every element of life to shape and form our compassion.

Grandma, your openness to all of life created in you a heart for service and hospitality. These beautiful expressions were manifested in various ways. For example, your kitchen table always had a flowery flannel tablecloth. This material was easy to clean up and readily available upon which to serve a meal at any time when guests or family came to visit. When my family and I would come to visit you, you were up at dawn with your apron on, busy making breakfast. We would just be done cleaning the dishes from breakfast and you were busy getting lunch and dinner prepared. Creating meals for others was an expression of your love and hospitality.

Sometimes while you were in the kitchen you would make meals for events occurring in the community, such as a funeral gathering. Other times, you were canning vegetables, preserving meat, making tortillas, *pastelitos,* etc., all items to have on hand for others who would come by or food you would share. Once your kitchen, house, or garden tasks were completed, you would be busy quilting or crocheting. These handmade items were not only for your home, but also gifts made for others. In your advanced age, your arthritic hands told the story of the years crocheting many items for those in your community and for loved ones. In all these activities, your apron remained on as an expression of love and service to those around you.

Grandma, wearing an apron each day was as habitual as your routine of prayer. You were a woman whose faith was centered on prayer. You prayed with your prayer books every day. I hold dearly the times you reverently showed me your prayer books. In those moments, I had to concentrate extra hard to follow your Spanish. For when you spoke about your love of God and Mary, your devoted heart would speed up your dialect as you expressed tender, passionate thoughts, though you were a soft-spoken person by nature. Your words always had depth and would linger like the aromas from your delicious meals.

You often referred to the Virgin Mary as Mother and were devoted to praying to her. I sensed the loss of your own mother strengthened your devotion to Mary, your advocate, protector, and a guide for your life. You prayed to her every day, several times in a day. Yet, you never drew attention to yourself when you were praying. With careful observation I saw the subtle movement of your fingers as you used them as rosary beads. In these prayerful moments, your hands became a different kind of instrument: A tool to pray for strength, guidance, protection, and wisdom for yourself and others.

Grandma, you are never far from my thoughts. Each time I put on an apron to make dinner, you are there. When I observe my small hands and all the ways I utilize them as tools in my life, you are there. When life brings struggle, change, sorrow, loss, and grief, I remember your words to accept and remain open, tender, compassionate, and earthed. Each time I get too ahead of my plans and wishes, I am reminded to hold the gift of today, hearing your voice say, "God willing." When I look upon your picture, I remember a woman of great strength, courage, resilience, service, tenderness, compassion, and a faith grander than your petite stature. Thank you, Grandma, for your faithful love, prayers, wisdom, and the many blessings you bestowed on to me.

Displaced in a Move

When I was about fifteen, my family moved from Grants, New Mexico to Wenatchee, Washington. We moved for my father's job. Wenatchee is a city in the center of Washington state. This move was my first time to live in a new environment, far away from my roots. My time in Wenatchee, although beautiful, proved to be a very confusing and challenging time. I experienced a dualism that impacted my sense of self, belonging, and being known.

Like the Columbia River that ran through Wenatchee, I felt like a river ran through my internal being, creating a divide within. Outwardly, I was engaged in our new community; I made friends and saw the positive aspects of our move. Yet, inwardly, I felt misunderstood, alone, and marginalized. I often masked my true self to be received and welcomed by those around me. I missed having extended family in proximity where I could be unapologetically and fully me. In Wenatchee, we were far from those who knew me the best.

While living there, I created friendships. However, the sense of connection was very different. Many of my classmates were living out what I envisioned for myself—what I would be living had we not moved. My classmates grew up going to elementary and middle school together. Many had connections to the high school in various ways. Their siblings attended or were present at the same high school, their parents worked in the district, etc. I was welcomed into friend groups, yet the connections between my peers were already long established. I understood what they were experiencing since that is what I left in New Mexico. Ultimately, throughout high school, I made good friends, participated in sports, had supportive teachers, and formed fun memories. However, I never integrated into established connections, nor was I fully seen or known.

I was also surprised to feel a division between my faith experience and what I had known within the Catholic tradition. For eight years prior, I had attended a parochial Catholic school. During that time, I attended daily Mass and was encouraged to engage and participate in the liturgy. When we got to Wenatchee, our Catholic Church was larger, fewer people looked like me, and the overall sense of the church felt more institutional than communal. The church experience was programmatic rather than alive and integrated into all aspects of life. I was never invited or encouraged to participate in the liturgy, which was 180 degrees from my elementary and middle school experience. Though we faithfully attended Mass every Sunday, it was the first time faith had become like everything else I was experiencing— compartmentalized.

Fortunately, some significant people came around while I lived in Wenatchee. Those individuals were our neighbors and some longtime, family friends. These relationships provided a sense of grounding and belonging. Our wonderful neighbors became our friends who wove us into their lives and stories. They were the people we saw most frequently, shared conversations, and had gatherings with. It felt good to be noticed and to experience a sense of investment by our neighbors.

I'm also thankful for our family friends who came to Wenatchee with us from New Mexico. My parents had a long history with these friends; one of their daughters was my godsister. They provided a sense of roots, culture, and a greater expression of knowing. We gathered with one another on weekends or holidays, and we often explored Washington together. Having my godsister come and spend time with us was always a thrill. She filled our home with laughter and fun. These family friends filled a void in a way that I desperately needed.

Moving to Wenatchee was an equally complex and significant move for my parents. They had not planned to leave New Mexico and be so far from extended family. Yet, they graciously reframed what they could not control and helped my brother and me see the good in the possibility this new move could bring. Understanding their hopes and wishes supported me while I navigated my Wenatchee years. However, it was sometimes challenging. Through it all, we leaned into our lives and created a sense of home for the years we resided there.

Like the Columbia River that divided the Wenatchee community, a split sensation occurred within me when we moved away, one that would take a long time to mend. Like the winters in Wenatchee, the feeling of being displaced created an impact like I was hidden and buried under layers of snow. This feeling took many years to diminish. Yet there were seasons where I experienced growth and springtime. Like the blossoming trees, our neighbors and friends were the fragrance of love and faithfulness. Over time, aspects of fruitful connections formed. The impact of being uprooted and acclimating to a life away from home gave me a heart to sympathize with, empathize with, and appreciate those who have experienced the uprooting dynamics of change.

Cotton Versus Polyester

I set out to create a string tie quilt.
My tia coached me through the process,
imparting to me her years of skill and wisdom and
sending me home with scraps of material from her collection.

Eager and excited to navigate this creative endeavor,
I dusted the sewing machine, which my mother gave me.
Hopeful yet hesitant to take that first step,
seeing the task through was overwhelming.

Beautiful material drew my creativity and gave me courage.
Soon, I was measuring, cutting, and sewing patches together.
In no time, I reached the final stages,
threading the string through three layers; sheet, batting, and patches.

Anticipation grew.
The taste of accomplishment drew near.
The last phase would entail folding the seams around the blanket's edges,
hand-stitching the border for a finish.

Yet, in this final stage, a significant error was revealed.
Sadly, I had made a rookie mistake.
The bottom sheet I used as my base
was polyester!

Polyester is not a quilter's friend.
It is a stretchy material.
A plastic, synthetic fiber that does not conform.
It doesn't lay even or straight.

Day after day, evening after evening,
I tirelessly ironed and pinned the edges down.
The polyester sheet would not lay flat
or hold any form I willed it to be.

With frustration and fatigue, I shouted,
"That is it! This polyester sheet will never do!"
With tears and a sense of defeat,
I took my seam ripper to unstitch the whole project.

A first-timer's mistake of using polyester versus cotton.
Polyester is an ideal material for sun protection and water resistance,
practical, functional, and convenient but it is not an organic fiber,
only an imitation.

Although it may look like cotton,
polyester does not function as its counterpart.
Cotton is an earthed material—
stable, absorbent, and breathable.

As I bitterly unstitched all my time and effort.
The dismantling process became a visceral experience.
Something deep within me was also becoming undone.
Metaphorically, I was unstitching aspects of polyester within me.

Polyester woven in the quilt of my life,
a protective mechanism for survival.

Functional, convenient, and at times imitational.
Non-breathable and moisture-resistant
unable to fully receive.

Genesis 2:7 says, "God formed humanity from the dust of the earth."
Like cotton, I am earthed:
stable, breathable, and absorbable.
Able to be receivable toward all of life, God, self, and others.

In this unstitching process,
truths were exposed to me:

> To embrace, release, receive, and love who I am entirely.
> To no longer be an impostor or imitation of my most authentic self.

Embrace all the patches of my life.
Remembering that I am also attached and sown into others.
Breathe, absorb, and receive the gifts of life,
Without fear, resistance, and protection.

Once I unstitched the polyester sheet,
I restitched my patches.
Bringing the three layers to a finish.
This time, using as the base
a cotton sheet!

How quickly and easily it all formed and came back together.
As I hand-stitched the edges,
metaphorically, I realized I was stretching aspects of cotton,
earth, truth, breath, and life back within me.

An inward labor of love and healing,
this first quilt turned out to be.

Part Five

Love and Life in a Spanish Song

A Saturday Morning Tradition Tribute to New Mexico Music

In scripture, Ecclesiastes 3: 1-2, 4 highlight that "for everything, there is a season, and a time for every matter under heaven: a time to be born and a time to die, a time to weep and a time to laugh, a time to mourn and time to dance." I have always appreciated this verse that gives depth to the both/and present in various conditions and seasons that unfold in our human existence. There is a time to embrace such expressions: weeping and laughing, mourning and dancing. Let each expression be part of the season they are meant to be without the pressure to rush or remain in one particular season. Listening to New Mexico music evokes seasons of tradition, celebration, dancing, and laughing. Wonderful Spanish songs written with poetic narratives, heartfelt gratitude, deep faith, a sense of home—songs central to many celebrations and the gift of music given from one generation to the next.

It is not common knowledge that New Mexico has a musical genre composed of several variations specific to regions within the state. For example, music from the northern part of New Mexico differs from that of the southern region. Songs are sung in Spanish, with a few songs woven with English and Spanish, Spanglish. New Mexico music is played across various radio stations. Most songs have fast tempos, lead guitarists, and provide simple tunes for dancing. Melodies are straightforward versus elaborate complex arrangements. Yet, the central aspect of all New Mexico music is the art of storytelling.

New Mexico music is rich in narrative expression. Many songs are rooted in folk stories and tributes. Many artists write about people and families in their close-knit communities. Some songs are uplifting, creating a spirit of joy, highlighting the importance of embracing life or simply being together and having a good time. Many songs tell stories of raw and honest aspects of life that people can connect with. Several songs are rich in spiritual faith and reflection. The song, "Cruz de Madera," ("Cross of Wood,") is an upbeat song that highlights a simple man's last wishes when he dies. He wants a cross of simplicity. He doesn't want anything special or grand to mark his death, nor does he want sadness or tears. His one request is to have a big party and a song sung through the night. This song encapsulated the essence of many New Mexico songs. It is a song written with beautiful, poetic, and authentic lyrics that draws you into a dance, to ponder, or to do both simultaneously, and it weaves the reality of life and death into a beautiful melody.

When a festival or family celebration occurs, sometimes a New Mexico band will be part of it. Weddings, anniversaries, graduations, family reunions, etc., are all opportunities for family and friends to listen and dance. A live band is a unique feature to celebrate milestone moments. Each time I hear the upbeat instrumental ballad "El Mitote/El Mosquito," I recall bands warming up as they played this song, building anticipation for the party and dancing to begin. Young children can't help but run around or jump up and down as the band rouses the crowd. There is a season to gather with family and friends to embrace the fullness of a special occasion and the gift of life. On such occasions, I treasure the memories of dancing with my father, grandfather, and other beloved family members, some living and others who have since died. I am thankful for the seasons when I jumped up and down, laughed, pondered, and danced with family and friends through the night.

New Mexico music has a generational aspect to many artists and bands. Growing up, my mom would play Al Hurricane record albums every Saturday morning as we did our chores. Al Hurricane was instrumental in forming what would become New Mexico music. He mentored and nurtured generations of New Mexico artists within his band, family, and others, and because of this, he is known as the Godfather of New Mexico music.

While doing chores, I enjoyed songs that featured Al Hurricane, Al Hurricane, Jr., and Tiny Morrie (Al's brother). One song in particular was my favorite: "El Pintor," (the painter) who painted eyes that would make you cry. Sometimes, New Mexico artists revitalize older songs in their own self-expression. "Ojitos Verdes," (green eyes), has been remade and refreshed many times. It is a song about a man who falls in love with a woman with captivating green eyes. The beautiful lyrics within this song evoke a season of love, longing, and sorrow.

The handprint of New Mexico music being passed down intergenerationally is also intertwined within my family. My cousin married a man named Manuel or "Manny." He played in a New Mexico band and could play the trumpet, guitar, and organ. Manny also had a clear, deep, and soulful voice. Each time he sang, it came from deep in his heart and spirit. He and my cousin loved to sing and passed the love of music to their children. One of their daughters, Monica, became a popular New Mexico artist known as AltaMoni.

One of my favorite albums produced by Monica is a collection of songs written about her family, aspects of her story, and faith. Monica sings a few songs on her album with her father, including a song written by Manny titled "Nunca Podre Comprende" ("I Will

Never Understand"). This song expresses Manny's deep faith and his understanding of God's love. Each time I listen to this song, I am drawn to special moments and memories of other family members singing together. Whether that was in a living room or a prayerful setting, I am filled with gratitude and sadness.

There are many voices of loved ones no longer alive that continue to sing in the echo of my heart. Listening to Monica and Manuel sing together holds those memories in a new season, demonstrating that the love of music and memories are handed down from generation to generation.

I love New Mexico music! It continues to evoke a sense of home, tradition, celebration, faith, and dancing. I have continued the tradition of doing Saturday chores with my family, listening to Al Hurricane and other artists. Often, we pause and dance around with joy and gratitude. Each time I listen to this music, I am filled with joy, appreciation, and memories of my family and loved ones. I am thankful for the poetic language and stories in New Mexico songs that highlight the various seasons and occasions in every matter under heaven.

Celebration of Life and Love

The song "Las Mananitas" (birthday or special occasion) and the narrative wedding march of "La Marcha de los Novios" ("Dance of the Bride and Groom"*)* are two songs that evoke life and love. Each holds a cultural tradition, narration, and celebration. One song honors someone's birthday or a significant moment, and the other is a narrative melody that ushers in a newly married couple or a couple celebrating an anniversary. Both songs create memories centered around life and love.

When I was young, I remember a significant anniversary that my tio and tia had. Several family members and I got up early to gather under their bedroom window. I remember it was a cool, crisp morning, and I was awed by the many family members who came to sing "Las Mananitas" to them. My tio and tia were surprised and deeply moved as they looked out their bedroom window. The energy was festive as our singing awoke them to their special day.

When "Las Mananitas" is sung to an individual or couple, it can catch them off guard. They realize they are being honored and celebrated when the song starts. The impact is still the same whether the song is sung a cappella, with instruments, or with a band. The person receiving the serenade understands they are being honored. It is a twofold moment of giving and receiving of love and affirmation. While still new to playing the trumpet, my son gave my mother a performance of "Las Mananitas" on her birthday. My mother was moved to tears even among the squeaky high cords and a few missed notes. She understood the effort it took for him to learn the song and the courage to play it for her to communicate love and appreciation.

Surprised by a chorus of loved ones or a solo person singing "Las Mananitas," it is worthy of attention. The beautiful lyrics encapsulate the essence of commemorating someone's life. The words joyfully name that all creation was aware and present to a person's birth. Birds sang, and the moon and the sun illuminated the day's arrival. Loved ones sing these poetic words to communicate their fondness, well wishes, and praise for life. My cousin's husband recently turned forty. Many people came to celebrate his birthday. As the evening progressed, family members who arrived to commemorate his birthday spontaneously started singing "Las Mananitas" to him. The singing came organically, and the heartfelt expression was sincere. Such an outward expression of gratitude was humbling. Tears and cheers filled the room—a vocal gift of acknowledging an influential person and the treasure of his life.

"La Marcha de los Novios" is an instrumental ballad played at weddings or anniversaries. This narrative melody is played to celebrate two lives joining or renewing their union in love. As a young girl, I was invited to participate in my cousin's wedding as her flower girl. I remember many things about this day, but this wedding march stood out the most. It is a traditional Hispanic/Latino dance that weaves together symbolic aspects of the marriage journey. Central to this dance is the joining of two individuals, their families, and their friends as they embark on their marriage voyage or as a renewal for a couple marking their anniversary. All the guests present for these occasions join the dance. Their participation represents the layers of accompaniment and support provided to the couple.

As the dance proceeds, it moves through different choreographed gestures representing elements that could arise in their marriage journey—navigating twists and turns, disagreements, and the need to build bridges in faithful love and commitment. The dance ends with the couple in the center, surrounded by their guests. In this space, the couple begins their first dance. From start to finish, the dance is full of energy and excitement. Everyone who participates claps their hands as they sway through the various sections of the dance. With whistling and *gritos* reverberating, emotion fills the space with extravagant joy and celebration. It is a fun and rhythmic dance that embodies the very nature of love and the extended beauty of communal affection to support a union.

"La Marcha de los Novios" always stirs my spirit with joy and gratitude. This song evokes memories of when I engaged in this dance for various cousins' weddings, the fiftieth wedding anniversary of my grandparents, and a beloved tio and tia on their sixty-fifth. Their anniversary was a beautiful, sacramental occasion to mark their love of family, community, friends, and one another. With family and friends gathered at their reception, my tio and tia youthfully moved through the song with buoyant spirits and radiant love—a day of affection and heartfelt celebration.

My fondness for "La Marcha de los Novios" deepened when this dance was part of my wedding day, played during the reception. Many of my family members traveled from New Mexico to Washington State to be part of our union. My future in-laws and guests had never experienced this tradition before. Honorably, my grandparents were the head couple to lead our dance. Everyone joyfully took on the invitation to embody this unfamiliar promenade. Cheers, clapping, and laughter filled the reception hall in a twofold commemorative experience. Captivation, wonder, and delight came over our guests as they enfolded into the last element: Everyone surrounded my husband and me for our first dance as a married couple. I remember the joy and love radiating around and within the two of us. We drank in the love present in one another and those encircling us.

Both sacred songs continue to evoke the celebration of life and love. Though varied in their context, they encapsulate joy, honoring, joining together, and marking a significant life or occasion. To this day, each time my husband and I hear "La Marcha de los Novios," we playfully move through the room until we are enfolded into one another in a dance. Each time, we remember our wedding day and the steadfast love that has only deepened throughout the years. Love and life, imprinted in a song.

Eres Tú, It's You
(An Inspired Duet)

Inspired by the New Mexico band Sorela and their version of the song "Eres Tú." Their upbeat style and beautiful harmony in this song danced in my head as I wrote this poem.

The image of the Divine present in the ocean, *eres tú*, it's you.
Strength in the tides pushing forward, pulling backward.
Mysterious aura hovers over the waters, *eres tú*, it's you.
Así, así, eres tú, so, so it's you.

Like the sea, the Divine mystery is constantly moving, *eres tú, eres tú.*
Water that is not stagnant but instead fully alive and active.
Shimmering reflective sunbeams shine on the water, *eres tú, eres tú.*
Así, así, eres tú.

The ocean's calm waters are inviting, *eres tú, eres tú.*
As my feet touch the sea,
your creative handprints, humanity and nature, in playful engagement, *eres tú, eres tú.*
Así, así, eres tú.

On occasion, the waters are calm and provide stillness, *eres tú, eres tú.*

Providing a tranquil silence.
Quieting the senses to listen to a peaceful proclamation, *eres tú, eres tú.*
Así, así, eres tú.

In this serene space, I see myself in the waters, *eres tú, eres tú.*
My reflection rippled in the sea.
The Divine sings affectionate words to me, *eres tú, eres tú.*
Así, así, eres tú.

You, dear one, are as vast as the sea, *eres tú, eres tú.*
Relish deep in the waters of my everlasting love.
You are the shimmering image reflected in the center of my eyes, *eres tú, eres tú.*
Así, así, eres tú.

A cherished masterpiece of my creation, *eres tú, eres tú.*
Part of nature's mysterious unfolding.
You are not stagnant but fully alive and in motion, *eres tú, eres tú.*
Así, así, eres tú.

Querida, listen as the waves invite you into a playful dance with me, *eres tú, eres tú.*
In the stillness, you have heard my voice calling you to wholeness.
Rest in tranquility and peace as you grow into your inner belonging, *eres tú, eres tú.*
Así, así, eres tú.

You and I will navigate the ocean waters within you, *eres tú, eres tú.*
Finding ease in their expansiveness and fullness.
Together, we will feed your confidence to amuse what is most true in you, *eres tú, eres tú.*
Así, así, eres tú.

Part Six

Nature's Reflective Wisdom

Earthed

This poem is dedicated to my ancestors and generations of family members who lived with the land.

Today I rose at sunrise—
another gift of the day.
I kiss my beloved, wash my face, and pour a cup of coffee.
As I dress, my body is a bit sore,
the physical fatigue reminds me
that each limb, joint, and muscle is functioning, essential.

Today I will ride my bike to the field.
A small field given to me by my father, and his father before him.
There is something remarkable knowing my hands
till the same soil of those who have come before me.
Such a gift imparted to me!
A field to cultivate life and vegetation.
A field that offers a larger understanding
and knowing that I too am earthed.

Vegetation from the earth is nourishment,
just as my unique gifts can cultivate substance for others.
Like the earth, I have limitations and imperfections.
Requiring constant compassion and goodness in every flaw,
and the release of unmerited expectations.

Each seed that is planted in the soil
falls into a journey of unfolding.
Trust and surrender, together,
are the key fertilizers to this undertaking.
This same process is needed for every seed sown
within my own life.
Patience is necessary.
Patience, always with myself.

The soil holds no secrets; it is honest to its lived experience.
Seasons of drought, great fertility, infection, fallow.
Memories of footprints of family running through
the harvest field.
Anxious and fearful energy released in the movement of
the field hoe.
Like the earth, I risk my own storytelling
and listen for the ongoing narration being lived around me,
hearing wisdom, wonder, and surprise.
The creative story of today,
grace present in every moment.

As I end the day, I set my boots upside down to dry.
The breeze that moves across the fields,
whispers farewell and offers well wishes as I pedal away.

Remember, you are earthed.
Always changing, vulnerable, resilient, a creative being.
You are a beautiful life woven within the ongoing parable of
creation.

A Single Red Leaf

Reflection on How Nature Mirrors Transition and Change

A single red leaf lay on the concrete walkway,
its vibrant, radiant color draws awareness.
Its bold, beautiful red contrasts against the gray,
commanding attention as if to say, "Behold, I am here!"

How did this single leaf get here?
There is no tree nearby to hint at its place of origin.
The wind has blown this red leaf,
as most leaves, in the season of falling away.

What must this leaf be feeling?
Perhaps lonely, lost, or confused.
Wishing it landed below the tree of its home
or perhaps in a nearby garden bed or farrow field.

Yet, here in this simple barren place, this leaf sits
aware that the natural movement of life to death will continue.
Decomposing as it must wherever it may land,
even in this place, without life or promise.

This beautiful red leaf will move through its life cycle.
Its color will lessen and soon fade away.
Breaking down into its natural role of being an organic mineral,
where the wind and rain will wash its traces away.

Yet, wondrously, nature by design will begin again.
The substance of all creation is to renew and rejuvenate.
Even this leaf that has settled in this seemingly desolate setting
has a story and contribution to make.

The minerals within this leaf will bring forth life.
It may be the one ingredient needed as it falls between the lifeless, cemented cracks,
deep in this forgotten place, not so easy to see.
Sun and rain will descend into the gap, feeding the hope of renewal.

This once-isolated leaf will combine with other living minerals hidden in the shadows—

> producing new growth that will emerge from between fractured places,
>
> bringing beauty, hope, and wonder, even in the most unexpected places, and
>
> bursting to the surface to announce again, "Behold, life is here!"

A Horse in a Field

A reflection on unearthing and living in the treasured essence of who we are created to be.

> *"The good road from above is like a hidden treasure a man finds buried in a field. He buries it back into the ground and is then happy to go and trade everything he had for that field."*
>
> *Matthew 13:44; First Nations Version: An Indigenous Translation*

A beautiful brown horse stands in a field.
At first glance and gaze, this horse is content and at peace,
Eating the lush, green grass that has been provided by the landscape.
The sun shines upon its body, providing warmth and a shimmering of highlights in its coat.

Yet this horse has a narrative, individually and ancestrally.
This horse has yet to remember who it was created to be,
the integral and interdependent aspects it brings to the whole,
unaware of the truth, treasure, and of the worth it contains.

The land remembers the essence and truth of this horse.
Aware of when all horses could roam and navigate the earth's terrain,

having offspring and traveling in accompaniment of others,
living in the organic rhythm of nature and in the larger circle of all things.

The land also knows an ancestral story of the horse in harmony with humanity,
when horses were held as part of a collective whole, a supportive creature, never to misuse.
Horses were part of stories, songs, and ceremonies,
understood and seen for their beauty, energy, healing, and symbols of freedom.

Yet, this beautiful brown horse has become detached from its narrative and
is now stuck between being hindered and being uncomfortable with the vast open terrain.
Trained for too long to fulfill a role, a task, or a goal.
Holding back the capabilities and instincts it unknowingly contains.

As the breeze blows across the field and dusk comes upon the earth,
a melody from the land emerges and spirits from long ago sing a chant.
This majestic creature slows and becomes attuned to this soothing song.
The Creator speaks within the chorus, calling forth remembrance and recall.

> *I have created you, my beautiful one, and I hear your voice,*
> *Along with the disorientation and unsteadiness you feel inside.*
> *For too long, you have forgotten to live in movement, in the now, today.*
> *Broken, trained, and burdened by the language of destination and quantification.*

Yet, you were created to move, jump, and prance in open spaces,
created to live with the land, among the community of kin and nations.
Listen to the land and how your ancestors speak of your majestic center,
Of your courage, endurance, strength, confidence—a valued gift to all you encounter.

It is time to return to your nature.
Balanced, connected, and in harmony,
you are a treasure, worth everything to claim, restore, and release.
Be free to reveal your wholeness as you embrace the Creator's good road within you.

Part Seven

Energy and Life in Playful Shimmer

The Legacy of the Bouncing Knee

In memory of my great-grandpa Laudes Sr., Grandpa Luciano, and uncles.

It all started with a man, a bouncing knee, and a rhythmic, native-like chant.
A man who would lovingly bounce his children, grandchildren, and great-grandchildren on his knee.
With great delight, each child would giggle and find joy.
Each focusing on the rhythmic chant he would sing as he bounced them on his knee.

This was my great-grandpa's way of bringing joy and delight to a small child.
I watched him as he bounced my younger brother on his knee, just as he did me.
I listened to his giggles and observed how my brother was drawn to the melody of my great-grandpa's rhythmic chant.

At this stage of his life, my great-grandpa was blind.
Yet, his awareness of a child on his knee was etched into his memory.
As he held my brother, I could see the expertise of a man who had

held and brought delight
to many of his loved ones and descendants.

My great-grandpa was always aware and eager to bring joy to those around him.
With his gentle nudges and playful tease, he could make them smile and laugh with delight.
Though blind in his later years, my great-grandpa always found a way to be engaged, especially if a young person was nearby.

I have a few tender memories of my great-grandpa
sitting on his living room floor or on the bench in his kitchen.
He enjoyed playfully mimicking my laugh.
He took great delight in exaggerating each pattern of my giggle making me laugh even more.
Although few words were exchanged, I knew I was dearly loved and cherished.

Later, my grandpa continued the bouncing knee and rhythmic native-like chant tradition.
Like his father, my grandpa bounced his children, grandchildren, and great-grandchildren.
Each child giggled joyfully while focusing on the
rhythmic chant he would sing as he bounced.

He, too, would be a grandpa who was always aware and present to those around him.
A grandpa who was always eager to be actively involved.
He played cards, watched basketball games, had meals, or fished with his delighted grandchildren.
In all things, my grandpa was swift to bring joy and love.

With his gentle nudges and playful tease, he could make you smile and laugh with delight.
And although few words of affection were shared,
you always knew you were much loved and cherished.

As the years passed, my uncles carried this spirit from their father and grandfather.
However, they did not bounce their children or grandchildren on their knees and sing the rhythmic, native-like chant.
Yet, they are uncles, fathers, and grandfathers
who are always aware and present to those around them.

Quick to be engaged and involved and create shared experiences together.
They, too, are swift to bring joy and love.
With their gentle nudges and playful tease, they can make you smile and laugh with delight.

This all started with a man, a bouncing knee, and a rhythmic, native-like chant,
a legacy of bringing joy and delight from generation to generation.
We carry memories of happiness and joy,
communicating through awareness and attentiveness:
We are cherished and dearly beloved.

The Joy and Delight of Physical Activities

Life can be busy, filled with expectations and demands. Participating in physical activity has been the one place I have found balance. It is the space where I let go of expectations, measurables, and the need for productivity. Having a physical outlet has allowed me to release what I carry in my head. Whether it's a good long walk, challenging run, or a group activity, I always come away from a physical activity feeling grounded, less worried, and able to see the goodness in my life. I am grateful for my health and for my physical abilities. I don't take these for granted and appreciate the vigor they bring to my life.

The physical outlet I enjoy most is running, though I wouldn't say I liked running at first. As a young girl, I became my dad's running partner, but I dreaded the days we were scheduled to run. Eventually, I grew to appreciate that running is a great way to get outside, experience mental release, and enjoy the natural endorphins brought forth from it. Running has been my vehicle to explore the various places I have lived and an avenue to find time to be alone. Running has been a catalyst for new adventures and a process that has created meaningful memories with family and friends.

There are seasons in life when running has been something I do for health and wellness, while other times running has been to reach a goal. Sometimes, running with a friend has been to meet a distance goal, to be companions while on a mountain trail, or as a shared space which often leads to meaningful conversations. These moments have been filled with joyful giggles, a healthy sweat, and even a few tears. Yet, time spent with another on a run has always been energizing and uplifting.

In addition to leisure running, I have participated in multiple marathons and half marathons. Each of these races required me to set out a running plan intended to build mileage and strength over the course of weeks leading to the race. Each time I committed to running a marathon or half marathon, the goal was always the same: I simply wanted to finish. My race times varied, sometimes fast and sometimes slow, yet each time I enjoyed being in a new location and running an unfamiliar route. I have always been in awe of the many other people participating with me in a race. Each person has trained and prepared to be in this experience for various reasons, purposes, and hopes. Absorbing that truth is both leveling and rewarding. Although each participant comes to the race as an individual, we become unified in the collective effort to reach our goals and become finishers.

While in Seattle, I had the opportunity to add biking and swimming to my exercise routine. These three activities led me to complete a series of sprint triathlons. This was even more meaningful when I convinced my mom to participate with me. Our first triathlon was the Danskin Women's Sprint Triathlon. My mom and I kept each other committed to meeting mileage goals and encouraged each other when we felt tired or anxious. Eventually when the race day drew near, my mom and I reverted to being giddy schoolgirls—we were both excited, nervous, determined, and confident that we were prepared to complete the race.

This event brought thousands of women together from different backgrounds, stories, ages, and physical abilities. The first heat consisted completely of cancer survivors. Seeing the cancer survivors participate in the race catapulted all the other participants to finish the race as both a personal and collective triumph. When my mom and I completed the race, we celebrated with the family members who had come to cheer us on. These memories hold a special place in my heart, not only for the experience of the race, but also the shared accomplishment with so many other incredible participants.

The joy and opportunity of new physical activities expanded when we moved to Okinawa, Japan. Here, I would be introduced to dragon boat racing. I decided to join an armed forces team called the Army Ladies Dragon Boat Team. Many on the team were new to dragon boat racing. Three nights a week, we gathered to master the necessary techniques and build endurance. Together, we developed the art of paddling and embraced the importance of teamwork as we built friendships and a sense of collective purpose. Technique and friendship were crucial as we prepared for the Okinawa Naha Hari Dragon Boat Race. Little did we know that all our preparation would lead to a historic outcome.

Okinawa hosts a traditional dragon boat race called Naha Hari. The Okinawan-style dragon boats used for this race are large, hand-carved wooden boats with decorative dragon heads facing the front and tails at the back. They are bright, colorful, and extremely heavy. Typically, dragon boats hold sixteen members, but the Naha Hari boat holds thirty-two paddlers. Our team had the fastest qualifying heat and therefore advanced to the finals. Thanks to our technical skills, precision, and unity, we outperformed the other two finalists and won the race. Spectators and other teams cheered, yelling, "Ladies, ladies, ladies!" The 2023 Army Ladies Dragon Boat Team would be the 49th Naha Hari winners and would become the first all-female team to ever be crowned champions.

It was amazing to participate in such a historic and culturally meaningful event. Being part of Naha Hari's history was remarkable. Spectators and other competitors gave us high fives and clapped for us as we exited the boat. Many spectators took pictures with us during the closing ceremonies. Sharing this with these amazing women, who were not only my teammates but also dear friends, was a once-in-a-lifetime experience.

Participating in physical activities has been a gift in my life. I have run through varied terrain, logged many miles, and even collected some bling along the way. My family has joined me on many of these adventures and this has only added to the depth and joy of the experiences. Who would have known that what began as a reluctant activity with my dad would lead me to so many valued and cherished memories.

Beautiful Butterflies

Each time I see butterflies, I am mindful of their transformative essence. They are creatures once hidden away in a chrysalis, awaiting a time to emerge to flutter among flowers, plants, or trees. Butterflies dance and move with pleasure and ease, seemingly resting in their true essence of belonging.

Butterflies symbolize many things: transformation, beauty, and rebirth. They embody endurance and hope. When their chrysalis walls fall away, they freely move in the world and channel their playful energy. As I have taken notice of butterflies, they seem to lure me into deeper reflection. Their beautiful wings and shimmering movement invite me to look further and consider if I can see myself. There is a butterfly instinct knitted, imprinted, and braided within the core of my being. I am eager to play, be engaged, experience growth, and be open to ongoing transformation. However, the struggles and worries of life can hinder these aspects. As a result, I often feel like I need to compartmentalize what is most authentic within me.

Thankfully, these butterflies whisper encouragement to me. As I lean in and listen, a tiny whisper quivers in the motion of their wings.

Hermosa mariposa, beautiful butterfly,
you are most alive when you are open and energized.
Full of courage and confidence, not worried about successful outcomes,
you genuinely enjoy with anticipation
the journey and process that is unfolding.
Curious about others, God, and even yourself.
These aspects are not meant to be fragmented,
sectioned, or pieced inside you.
You are fluent in the dance we create.
You understand how to bask and bathe
with great delight to everything and everyone around you.
With wonder and strong intuition, you live holistically.
In your authentic self, you are alive in your instinctive butterfly reflection.
Not in segments of your life but in every aspect, in every detail of who you are.

Thank you, beautiful butterflies. I do see and know the fabric of myself reflected in you. Thank you for your determined faithfulness to call forth the essence of my true self so that I can be at ease in my entire knowing and belonging. Hermosa mariposa, you are fully present in me.

Part Eight
Essential Truth

Purple Flowers

Death is something people often fear or choose to ignore. Yet, death is present in life, every day. Whether we entertain or give it much attention, it doesn't change the actuality of death. From a young age, I was taught that death was not a reality to be anxious about or to fear. I was taught, instead, to acknowledge that death is part of life.

My father first showed me as a little girl death in nature, particularly around animals. If a small bird fell out of a nest or a car hit an animal, he brought death to my attention with gentleness. He did not shield me from death just because I was young. Through the years, I learned that when death arrives, it requires tenderness, space for authentic emotions to be shared, support, and compassionate spirits and hearts no matter the cause or circumstance around the death.

Growing up, I enjoyed getting together with my extended family. When the family gathered around the kitchen table, they talked and shared stories. In those settings, I was either at the table or just far enough away to hear what was being discussed. Conversations often moved around trivial aspects of life, events, or updates, and sometimes, the dialogue was silly, but at other times, the subject matter took a serious tone. Each time, those at the table spoke authentically, no matter the subject.

Listening to family members being honest, vulnerable, and emotionally exposed gave me a framework for navigating life's uncertainties. By being forthcoming and transparent with their thoughts and emotions, they modeled how to own and hold their authentic selves. Exposing what was true within their hearts and spirits reflected a more profound sense of knowing themselves, God, and others. This transparent way of being was organically embodied in all aspects of life, especially when death came to a loved one or someone in the community.

Death can be heartbreaking. Whether the death is expected or unexpected, sadness is always present. As a young girl, I experienced the death of family members and those within my community. Witnessing how family and friends grieved and provided empathetic support to each other was formative. Death brings many emotions. Being able to name and claim emotions honestly requires safety, compassion, and understanding. From a young age, I understood that expressing raw and real thoughts without judgment was essential to allow healing. The importance of authentic sharing remained valid as I experienced death firsthand and supported others in their grief and loss.

Compassion and loving support are bedrock when a death occurs. These factors are especially essential when a death occurs by self-infliction. This kind of death is always tragic. In my formative years, a very young person took their life. I did not know them personally, but my family and those in the community loved them and their family very much. The conversations around such a death were the first that I would behold. Yet, this tragic experience stayed with me and impacted how I arrived to support others as they faced the same circumstances.

When death comes, there are often no words or answers to comfort those left behind. There are no comments or explanations to answer why. When someone dies, it is essential to honor and celebrate their life and address the absence left behind. When someone takes their life, the weight of these dynamics can bring collapsing sorrow. Feelings of shame, regret, helplessness, and even a sense of injustice flood the soul. Shouldering such pain and grief will take a community or small group of others to extend understanding, grace, compassion, and love without judgment.

This poem highlights what was modeled to me when supporting a family and community in death.

The purple flowers
give witness to layered grief
never forgotten

A young person's life
full of beauty and promise
ended abruptly

Family saddens
questioning what was the cause
of isolation

No known reason found
to comfort the broken hearts
only confusion

Community, church
consider their given roles
addressing despair

Honoring a life
so dramatically taken
without playing God

Trusting instead in
God's tender hold of the heart
faithful mercy, love

Staying authentic
community together
to grieve and to mourn

Providing comfort
no room for any judgment
simply together

Shouldering the grief
will allow the heart to heal
through seasons and time

Faithful companions
this community will be
healing for the one

Healing for them all.

One Word

Imagine for a moment that you are in the hospital. Your medical team has informed you that you have a life-threatening disease. This disease is located in your brain, and as a result, it will impact your short-term memory. This condition will create a pattern of forgetting why you are hospitalized. Every other day, you will relive the experience of being told you have a life-threatening disease impacting your short-term memory. On those days, you will experience fear, confusion, worry, and stress as if it were the first time you have heard such news.

While serving as a spiritual care provider, I met a patient named Santiago, whose medical condition was this reality. Due to his condition, he would be told why he was in the hospital and about his condition every other day. Santiago was alone in the hospital with no family or friends to support or assist in his memory lapses. A sense of isolation only increased his distress.

The first few times I visited Santiago were usually on days of lapsed memory. During these initial visits together, I allowed him to weep, lament, and grieve his diagnosis and condition. As I attended to his worries and concerns, I discovered that Santiago found strength in prayer and scripture. Each time we met, I prayed for him. I also started writing scripture that he found comforting on paper so he could read it when he felt down. Soon, I posted these verses on the wall in his room. I hoped seeing familiar phrases would comfort him when he experienced confusion and fear.

As I continued meeting with Santiago, I noticed that a specific word had deep meaning for him. A word that, when spoken, appeared to be rooted within his long-term memory. When Santiago shared the depth of this word, he always had a story. Sometimes, it was how this one word helped him in different decisions in his life, circumstances, and challenges he faced. Occasionally, it was connected to significant people that he admired and loved. Since his long-term memory was still fresh and sharp, bringing this one word to the surface gave him grounding. It also served as a beautiful bridge to get to know Santiago as a person beyond his medical condition. Knowing more of his story allowed his medical team to take a more holistic approach to supporting his medical needs. This bridging also allowed Santiago not to feel alone.

Santiago recalled times he experienced sorrow, joy, pain, loss, brokenness, forgiveness, and isolation. He expressed remorse for his decisions that caused an estrangement between him and his loved ones. Yet, through this one word, he could also claim the very essence of what was still true about who he was. Santiago was someone who loved and was loved. This illumination was transformative as he faced confusion and illness. Naming this truth was also restorative.

One day, while shopping at a bookstore, I found a small rock with Santiago's word inscribed on it. I purchased the rock and took it to him. The inscribed rock became a source of strength for him. Although he would continue to suffer from short-term memory loss, somehow, this one word on this rock kept him grounded through each memory lapse. The brutality of his short-term memory loss was hard to watch at times. I often felt helpless as I held his fear and distress with tenderness. Yet, I also witnessed the power of one word to guide the fear and worry in a different direction.

I routinely visited Santiago while he was in the hospital. I am not sure he ever remembered or made a connection to who I was by my assigned role. As time went on, he often called me mija, a Spanish word of endearment and knowing. We found a kinship through the telling of stories. Storytelling gave Santiago respite and the ability to find reprieve from fear and disorientation. It allowed him for a moment not to become paralyzed by the harshness of his condition. Eventually, Santiago was transferred to another care facility. With his belongings gathered for his departure, he hugged me goodbye. In his hand was his rock.

My time with Santiago caused me to ponder what word or phrase would be rooted in the stories of *my* life. What word or phrase would give me grounding if the roles were reversed between Santiago and me? Would there be a word that could draw stories, events, or people from my past? Could one word give me meaning, grounding, and strength? The power of one word may allow me to slip through the trap of fear and confusion to find peace, even for a moment. Could I come up with a summative word to illuminate what had been true about me: that I was someone who loved and was loved? Maybe a phrase or word that would illuminate my understanding of love?

In reflection, that word for me would be *mi hijita*. Mi hijita was a word my parents and relatives used for love and endearment. I was called this name as a little girl and as an adult. It has meaning for me related to belonging, acceptance, welcome, and being known. If I were to hold one word in a time of trial or trauma, this would be the word. It sums up what it means to be cared for and safe. As I have reflected on Santiago and his one word, I am so grateful for spending time on his journey. It was a meaningful connection and experience that has continued to stay with me and has shaped my pondering on what I would hold as my word.

A Different Kind of Emmaus

This reflection is inspired by the scripture story of Jesus encountering two people on the road to Emmaus (Luke 24:13-35). In this story, two individuals experienced grief, confusion, and even a loss of hope. Death entered their narrative, and they were unmasked as they processed aloud their sorrow. In this setting, they encountered Jesus, but it appeared they did not recognize him. They were vulnerable and honest with their thoughts as they risked sharing their authentic and current reality. Jesus listened and engaged them with words that began to reframe their lived experience, including their current grief and their prior seeds of hope. As powerful as words and dialogue can be, we often live experientially. The words Jesus offered and their authentic expressions came more fully alive when they sat together for a meal. In the breaking of the bread, they transitioned through their current state and entered the embodied reality of knowing and being known honestly and authentically. This familiar experience solidified their whole selves and opened their eyes to what they were experiencing and whom they were experiencing it with. In this embodied moment, they recognized and realized that Jesus was in their midst.

Too often, we engage with one another in the opposite of this story. Instead of openly sharing and allowing others to enter our vulnerable spaces, we are more likely to maintain a safe distance, even among our closest friends and family. The scripture story of the road to Emmaus might offer an invitation to a different option and way of being. What if a slight alteration to some of life's experiences could bring about a significantly different encounter? Death, grief, and fear are often subjects that are held privately. The challenge and gift of the Emmaus story is to offer a different option for moving in and through death, grief, and fear. The willingness to transcend the rules may allow us to see and encounter one another more holistically and perhaps even see the Divine within our midst.

Here is a reflection on the courage to live the transparent essential truth of the road to Emmaus.

> You see a small grouping of people you love walking along a path. You run to catch up to them and listen to their conversation. They are worried and afraid. They share their thoughts aloud, but each holds back their true thoughts and feelings. Like a theater production, they each play parts. They are being mindful to use words on the script carefully, each staying in their assigned character, unwilling to reveal their authentic voice.
>
> You hear their conversation and offer comfort, encouragement, and support. You love these individuals dearly. You are familiar with them. You are someone who has walked with them faithfully for many years. Before long, everyone declares that they are getting hungry. They decide to find someplace to sit down and share a meal. Eating a meal together has always been easy and comfortable for them. It is something they enjoy doing together. Yet "breaking bread" together is something they have never done.
>
> Bread at meals has always been cut, divided, and sectioned into perfectly divided, precise pieces for each person. Safe. Fair. Controlled. Yet, on this day, you take the bread at the table, and with both your hands, you break the bread apart. No knife, no

object. Fully embodied, messy. You break the bread into pieces for each person. The pieces are not precise but uneven. The whole scene is chaotic. Exposed.

Once the bread has been broken, truth is spoken—the opportunity to acknowledge and address the undercurrent in every interaction they have had together.

You say,

I am exhausted! This theater production we have been performing can no longer go on. The endless expectations and fear of performing only in our set roles are not okay and never have been! The roles given to each of us have been suffocating, life-taking, heavy, and restrictive. It's not okay that we have not been encouraged or supported to explore other possibilities. We have yet to be allowed to speak or share our assertions to bring a change. It is not okay that we have been required to remain confined to our given roles, spoken or unspoken. Bounded.

Then you pause. With tears and words of compassion, you say,

No more! I love you all. But no more! It's time we all live in truth and to leave these roles we have all been performing in. It's time we eat and be people who break bread together as beautifully imperfect, broken, and searching souls. Let's embrace holistic nourishment for one another. Let's be transparent.

We have always been devoted to one another. It's time to reveal who we truly are. We are no longer characters stuck to roles or set scripts. Instead, let's be who we are: individuals with self-expression, longing to be seen, known, and understood. No longer familiar but recognizable! This long-lived production must conclude. Let us be people who break bread together and risk letting our true selves be revealed.

Part Nine

To Love and Serve

The Ursuline Sisters' Handprint

I attended a Catholic parochial school from first through eighth grade. It was a school started by the monastic order of the Ursuline Sisters. During my attendance, there were a few Ursuline Sisters who still taught and held administrator positions. For eight years, they shaped my education, faith, Catholic lay ministry, and service. Each of these ingredients remained formative in my life and faith.

Some parochial schools are considered strict, rigorous, and challenging, and if you add actual nuns into the setting, the stories only intensify. In truth, school was demanding, rigid, and stringent. Mastering educational concepts, study skills, and high standards was expected. I ebbed and flowed with high achievement and with significant failure. Sometimes, that created extra stress and strain. Yet, there were also times when I felt uplifted, encouraged, empowered, and I knew learning was fun. Some of the skills instilled in me are no longer taught or mastered by my children: memorization of multiplication factors, diagramming sentences, and keeping a small flip notebook to write down daily homework. On the other side of that coin, my kids never stayed in from recess to write dictionary columns or write one hundred times, "I will not talk in class." Since I was a repeat offender, I mastered using two pencils instead of one to move through the one hundred lines quickly. If my hands were bigger, I may have tried three!

My faith formation had various experiences of integrated learning entwined throughout my eight years of school. One way was through the Catholic liturgy. We began each day attending Mass. I attended Mass 1,440 times in those eight years (not including Sunday or feast days). That's some serious church time! Luckily, the Ursuline Sisters made this experience less tasking by utilizing it as an opportunity to cultivate a culture of early lay ministers. Each year as a class, we were given new roles to participate in and be engaged in the liturgy: bringing up the gifts, being lectors or altar servers, singing in the choir, or cleaning the church.

Along with these participatory roles, the sisters did an excellent job making the liturgical calendar of seasons and feast days relevant. They did this through music, sensory elements and narration, and physical activities that brought the liturgical season and feast days to life. To this day, certain songs, smells, stories, images, or colors in Mass take me back to my childhood years. For example, the song "Only a Shadow" was a song I sang for my First Holy Communion. Each time I hear that song, I am a second grader in my white dress walking down the aisle of the church, making sure I stepped on the brown tiles, not the beige ones, to be in sync with the whole procession. The handprint of integrative learning of the liturgy given to me by the Ursuline Sisters is still woven into my life as an adult. If you come to my house over the advent season, you will discover a wooden holy family hidden above a door or along a baseboard as they travel through our home to find the manger before Christmas.

Although we experienced the liturgy daily in Mass, the Ursuline Sisters instilled in us that the liturgy was not limited to church buildings. Faith and being an incarnational witness to the world began in how we loved and served those around us. That included our classmates. Traveling with the same twenty-five students from first through eighth grade made that task at times seem unattainable.

These classmates were my closest friends, periodically my worst enemies, and eventually future crushes as we journeyed through the years. Service to one another meant navigating the joys and struggles with one another. This dynamic of fostering a community was also challenging and trying on our teachers. In a rare moment, I witnessed a sister lose her patience. She sharply yelled at a fellow student who was behaving foolishly and said, "Renee, stop acting like a jackass!" Her statement created the shock needed to grab this student's attention and a moment as a class we would talk about for a long time. Luckily, by staying in faithful service to one another, we did manage to grow and strengthen our bonds. By the time we were seventh and eighth graders, we were each other's dearest and closest friends.

There were other opportunities to serve and be an incarnational witness to others outside of the classroom. In my seventh and eighth grade years, we served as the choir for many funerals. Serving in this role was always a meaningful and tender experience. Providing a service to a family in mourning was impactful. It fostered the perspective that on any given day, one person can experience life and joy, while another person or family may experience loss and grief. This formed within me the creative understanding that life and death walk hand in hand each day.

As seventh and eighth graders, we performed a few service fundraisers. We were also invited to the sisters' home to dust their living areas. Going to dust for them was one of my favorite experiences. It was fun to go with a few friends to dust their furniture and see where they lived. It made our connection to them different as we witnessed them as people who had kitchens, bedrooms, televisions, etc. Sometimes, they shared stories about themselves and offered us some cookies. It was enlightening to see them as ordinary people, hear their stories, and see them beyond their given roles at school.

The Ursuline Sisters fostered and cultivated integrative faith deep within me. In eighth grade, I received the Sacrament of Confirmation. For eight years, the seed to love and serve God by loving and serving others became real for me. It became the confirmation purpose for my life. This seed only grew and flourished as I lived that out in various ways. The handprint of the Ursuline Sisters shaped my love for the liturgy and cultivated a faith that is still relevant and alive. The Ursuline Sisters also inspired my draw to monastic formation and mystic contemplation. I am forever thankful for them. They fostered a faith in me that sees and experiences God in all things as well as the ongoing call to love and serve God by loving and serving others in all things.

Love and Serve

When I was in eighth grade, I received the Sacrament of Confirmation. On this day, I remember naming that I wanted to live my life loving and serving the Lord. That desire has been lived out in various ways throughout my life. I have brought the heart of love and service to specific roles as youth minister, campus minister, community service teacher, spiritual care provider, and spiritual director. Yet, I have also lived out love and service in the role of a barista, coach, neighbor, and friend. I confess that in my earlier years of living from my heart to love and serve others, I was dutiful to the application of these two concepts rather than understanding that love and service are an embodied way of being. I'm sure after I write and read this in a few years' time, I will have a new depth of understanding what it means to love and to serve self, God, and others. Love and service is an ongoing process and practice. It requires a posture of openness to allow encounters with others to expand and grow what loving and serving means to me.

Some encounters that shaped me during my pursuit and participation in this process have come in some unlikely forms. There have been more than a few, but some have stood out, in part due to their contribution to my journey and the timing with which they came. They can be reduced to a simple description of a colleague in a coffee shop, a high school student, and a group of hospital patients who had no place to call home. Their impact and what I have received have been much more than just those simple descriptions.

After the birth of my first son, returning to the traditional workplace proved more challenging than I had anticipated. There were many contributing factors to this, but the outcome was that I ended up looking to an entirely different field for my next job. I was able to secure inexpensive, half-day childcare and went to work for a large coffee company based in Seattle. As a barista in a downtown high-rise office building, I interacted with many different people from many different backgrounds. I even served the owner and founder of this coffee company a latte one day. My manager let me know after the fact that I had done a wonderful job because this particular customer had a reputation for letting employees know if they had made a mistake.

My coworker was a person who had been labeled by many as having an alternate lifestyle. He shared experiences of being judged, excluded, and labeled in ways that were not meant to uplift. As I got to know this individual, I became aware of just how wonderful people can be along with how caring, how giving, how interested, and how perspectives deeply change one's understanding and awareness. I found myself in the fortunate position of being given and shown kindness in unexpected ways. I received acceptance and, in turn, was shaped to become more accepting. I experienced being trusted by someone who had experienced distrust more than trust. My time working for this corporate giant proved incredibly impactful, not because of the green apron or the title I held, but because I learned about friendship, acceptance, diversity, and the power of sharing in another's journey (and a cup of coffee sometimes helped too).

Some years later, I went to work in the education field at a private Catholic high school. As a campus minister, I was charged with running annual retreats for juniors and seniors. I recruited, selected, and helped train students who would lead such retreats. The process of inviting students to share portions of their story with their peers inevitably created avenues to hear and know more of who they were. One student in particular had grown up in what most would consider a privileged home. His parents were both very successful according to the world and he had many cousins and extended family who were shining examples of what everyone would hope to be. This student was not big in stature or personality. He did not stand out from the crowd in any particular way. He was already wrestling with the idea that maybe he could not measure up to the expectations and patterns he saw around him in his family.

This student was already cultivating seeds of self-doubt, worry, lost hope, and criticism. As we dialogued about who he was, our conversation managed to unearth the reality that who he was was already enough. He was created to be uniquely himself, and the gifts he had inside were not less than the gifts of those he saw around him. He was who he had been *made* to be. As the weeks went on and the retreat approached, the depth of our conversations had increased. I realized that as I was sharing with this teenager all the many truths I hoped he would embrace, I too needed to absorb the depth of these words. This embrace of who God had made me to be needed to transcend what I was doing and attempting to do for others. I realized through the story of this high school student, that I too was created to be who I was and that the gifts I possessed were perfectly tailored to me.

Following my time in the education world, I transitioned to become a spiritual care provider at a level one trauma hospital in downtown Seattle. This hospital served the needs of the entire population from not only Washington, but also the surrounding states as well. This hospital took in all patients, regardless of their ability to pay. I completely resonated with this mission and looked forward to going to work each day in anticipation of who I might have the privilege of encountering. My team served a very vulnerable population. Some asked me if I was constantly scared to go to work with "those people." *Those people* were just people. They each had a story, and although trauma and tragedy had plagued them (maybe more than others), they were people, nonetheless. In fact, I came to see that their trauma and tragedy had allowed them the gift of showing their real selves with much less effort than I had ever allowed myself to know.

One day I was leaving work and as I passed through the massive front doors of the emergency room, I encountered a trio of friends who were awaiting placement in transitional housing that would come when they were well enough and healed enough to leave the hospital. They were gathered on the corner, in hospital gowns and wheelchairs. They had managed to procure a few cigarettes and were partaking in an evening smoke. As I approached them, I recognized who they were and was happy to offer a smile. They however were not content with returning a simple greeting or cordial hello. They stopped their conversation and with raised hands greeted me with, "Hey, it's Miss Adrianne! Have a great night! See you tomorrow!"

As I waved and passed by, my heart received their gift of genuine acknowledgment. This moment still brings tears to my eyes. I was *seen* by them, and they took the time to value and recognize me. What a gift! I had the opportunity in that moment to experience the power of being seen and valued and welcomed. This experience helped me to lean into the deep gift that each person is, and at our core we all benefit from being authentically seen and acknowledged.

As an eighth grader getting confirmed all those many years ago, how could I have known or anticipated where my journey would take me in my pursuit to love and serve the Lord? All these years later, I remain open to encounters with others to expand and grow what it means to love and serve.

Love Over Hate, Faith Over Despair

Tribute to Sister Dianna Ortiz

Sister Dianna Ortiz impacted my life at a very young age. She influenced my desire to love and serve others. She faithfully maintained a heart of love and service despite the horrific trauma that significantly changed her life. Sister Dianna Ortiz embodied the fullness of what it means to be incarnational love and grace in all things. She spent her life serving those on the margins who are often forgotten. She brought awareness to the plight of others and advocated for their dignity and voice.

I met Sister Dianna Ortiz when I was in grade school. She was an Ursuline Nun who lived in my hometown. She became a nun at the age of seventeen. I remember the day she walked into my school. She was young, vibrant, full of life, graceful, confident, and stunning (inside and out). She was a beautiful nun! She was kind, welcoming, approachable, and personable. Her devoted faith was attractive and alluring. She spoke passionately about the importance of education and encouraged us to appreciate the gift of learning, our teachers, and to put our best efforts into our studies.

As Sister Dianna continued to spend time at our school, she encouraged us to grow in our love and understanding of God. She shared that the way we experience God's love is in the way we love and serve others. When she came to our school, she shared that she was preparing to be a missionary to Latin America. While she was there, she would be a teacher for the Indigenous Maya children in a village in Guatemala and serve those on the margins. Sister Dianna went to Guatemala while the country was experiencing a civil war.

While she was in Guatemala, we exchanged a few letters. Her letters were a treasure to receive as she described her love of teaching, the people, and of God. She always encouraged me to continue to grow in my faith, reminding me that to love God was to love and serve others. I appreciated each of her beautiful letters and was thankful for the time and effort she took to correspond. I was also heartbroken when what unfolded in her life erased all memory and connection to those she knew and loved, including me. On November 2, 1989, Sister Dianna's life personally and vocationally would be forever altered.

On that day, members of the Guatemala military abducted, detained, raped, and tortured Sister Dianna for twenty-four hours. Ultimately, she was targeted for working with the Indigenous community. The ordeal impacted her memory and connection to those she knew before her abduction. She spent several years rebuilding her life, including going through intensive counseling. She eventually settled in Washington, DC, where she became an advocate for survivors of state-sanctioned violence.

Sister Dianna often stated that her abduction was not uncommon for many Guatemalan civilians in 1989. What was unusual was that she survived and was able to reveal details about what had happened to her. She often commented that the miracle of her life would forge a new mission for her out of this unspeakable horror and that mission was to create the Torture Abolition and Survivors Support Coalition International (TASSC). Sister Dianna spent a decade as the executive director of this organization. TASSC is headed by torture survivors who seek to unite and magnify the voices of other tortured victims. TASSC also helps torture survivors repair and restore their lives. TASSC and Sister Dianna were recognized in countless awards and publications for their work in support and advocacy for torture victims in over sixty countries. Sadly, she died of cancer at the age of sixty-two on February 19, 2021.

Sister Dianna is forever etched in my heart and memory. She did not remember me after her abduction and torture, yet I remembered her and followed her life and mission. I have often sought her companionship and wisdom in my prayers. Below is a poem written in tribute to her, a collection of thoughts and words she stated throughout her life, including in her letters to me.

Words of Wisdom from Sister Dianna Ortiz

Life is not always clear.
Questions we hold are not always resolved.
Forgiveness is necessary, yet forgiveness isn't something we can understand.
That is up to God.

Healing wounds is a process.
Often, with steps going forward, there are many more steps going back.
Yet, love is consistent, steady, and relentless in the healing process.
Rest in love.

Prayer is essential,
central to giving our faith grounding.
As we live our lives, loving God is to love others.
Ground everything in prayer and faith.

Laughter is a must.
Find joy and delight in small things.

A heart of gratitude woven with giggles is key.
Keep this always.

Hold balance
between reading Scripture and reading the newspaper.
Each will guide how we participate and serve the world.
Scripture continues on, living parables present every day.

Be tenderness filled with strength.
Stand in the suffering of others.
Bring love and hope to those who suffer unjustly.
Do not be a bystander; replace injustice with justice.

Hold those in power to account.
Advocating to fix broken systems that impact the poor and vulnerable unjustly.
Systematically, politically, nationally, and globally:
Speak out! Stand With!

We are called to love and care for the hurting in the world.
When we are too focused on our own self-interest or concerns, there is no room for others or the poor.
We can't hear God's voice when we are focused only on ourselves.

We are all part of the human family,
here to see and care for the most vulnerable among us.
Hearts must be willing and open to understand the plight of others.
We need to see how God sees.

To love God is to love others.
Maintain communities of prayer and fellowship.
Champion the needs of others.
Reframe our eyes to see Jesus in our midst.

Part Ten

A Soul Is at Home

Roots from a Little Mountain Town

A common question often asked is, "Where are you from?"

I say, "I am from New Mexico. Born and raised in a small mining town west of Albuquerque named Grants. Yet, my roots and lineage are from northern New Mexico in a little mountain rancher community called Vadito."

This community is a vessel that contains my ancestral history, culture, extended family, and the foundations of my faith. It may be small geographically, but this location holds a sense of well-being that only my heart and soul understand. Each time I visit, a deep sense of belonging stirs my heart, the comfort of simplicity expands, and the fragrance of love and faith penetrate my spirit.

Vadito is one of many little rancher communities in northern New Mexico. Each has a long historical tradition of Spanish and Indigenous cultures living with each other and with the land. Those who lived in these communities typically had large families. Eventually, people intermarried with those who lived in nearby towns or within the mountain communities. This dynamic is part of my parents' lineage. As a result, Vadito holds both my mother's and my father's rooted family history. When I am introduced to someone in Vadito, I am introduced as the *hija* (daughter), *nieta* (granddaughter), or *bisnieta* (great-granddaughter) of my parents or an extended relative. Being presented this way instantly places me in a broader family context and knowing. To have myself and my children framed in a more comprehensive family history is honoring and provides a deep sense of belonging, intimacy, and an understanding of home.

Vadito is a place of incredible simplicity and practicality. Living with the land naturally created a mindset of waste not, want not. Everything given from the earth was a gift to value, not held as a commodity. Living in rhythm with nature and the seasons created an interconnectedness. Food that was produced was utilized resourcefully and never taken for granted. Resources were shared, preserved, or dried so as to not waste anything. Like all things grown in a specific area, produce has a unique taste due to the soil and climate. Plum trees grown in Vadito produce plums with a distinct sweet and tart flavor. Because of the high elevation and dry climate, when they are dried, they become dense prunes. These prunes hold their form when turned into pie filling. This sweet, tart, firm, and chewy pie filling creates the best plum *pastelitos* (prune pies). Each time I bite into a plum *pastelito*, I am instantly transported back to my grandma's kitchen as a young girl, enjoying having pie in the day or late at night. Goodness and sentiment all in one bite.

Houses in Vadito are built to be functional. Wood stoves still serve as a primary source for heat and cooking. Finding creative ways to repurpose familiar items is also a common practice. My grandma used old coffee cans as pots for her plants. Worn-out jeans, retired clothing, and old flannels became fabric for quilts. With contributions from my great-grandma, grandma, tias, and cousins, there is not a bed that does not have a handmade quilt on it. As a young girl, I remember crawling into bed at my grandma's house with layers of quilts to keep me warm. After creating a warm spot within the cold sheets, the weight of all the quilts kept me motionless and cozy. As I have stepped into the tradition of quilt making, I often feel my relatives with and around me. Their tiny hands mirror mine as I cut, stitch, and lay out material. I now understand their hearts as they brought together pieces of fabric to create quilts of warmth and love for family and friends. There is truly something special about an original handmade gift made for a specific person or loved one.

Each time I visit Vadito, I am showered with love, hospitality, and joy and with welcoming spirits, lots of hugs, and kisses. My family quickly provides nourishment, comfort, and restoration. Slowing down to be with one another comes naturally as we sit together for a meal. With food spread across the table, conversations turn into stories and reflections, with occasional moments of tears or laughter. It is in this context that some of the best lessons of life have been given. Here's where everyone tells of their navigating the trials of work, weathering conflicts with family or neighbors, supporting those who are sick or alone, and balancing the needs of older parents while also being active with children or grandchildren. Through authentic sharing, life lessons and wisdom are naturally imparted.

Their love is also felt in the alluring aroma of faith. When a candle is lit or blown out in a room, a scent lingers in the air, pronouncing the candle's contribution. No words or attention are needed, just the subtle fragrance and awareness that a candle is in the room. This analogy is also found in my extended family's language and fragrance of faith. Their expression of faith is woven and quietly integrated into their very way of being. It is present in their hospitality, gratitude, humility, generosity, joy, and contemplative, prayerful spirits. This alluring fragrance of tenderness and grace is uplifting and comforting.

A beloved tio and tia of mine always made God approachable and playful. They held a deep devotion to their faith, were lectors in church, and served their community in many formal and informal ways. I remember witnessing them in a variety of settings and they always seemed to seek out joy, find a connection to faith, and they were quick with a smile and laughter. Faith and fun were woven together in equal measure—a sweet scent I often longed for when I was not with them. A phone call to my tio was all I needed to keep life's trials in balance. With his simple words of encouragement and a playful tease, I always felt embraced across the miles. It served as a reminder that I was beloved, and that God was with me.

So where am I from? The short answer is Grants, New Mexico. However, Vadito is the home of my roots. Simplicity, family, and faith are the essential aspects of this community. These beautiful details have remained in those who still live there and are contained within my extended family. They continue to model how to value nature and community. These lessons continue to inform how I navigate life's challenges and support family members who live far away. The essence of Vadito and the fragrant love of all who once lived there is carried on to the next generation. I am grateful for the many handprints in my life, both the living and long departed and for those who have shaped my perspective of belonging, simplicity, family, and faith. All aspects were planted and cultivated by generations of people in this small mountain town.

Thousand Square Feet on 138th Street

There is something valuable in holding an abundance mindset. This mindset is that there are more than enough resources for everyone when we are willing to share and offer to share with others. Our first home on 138th Street held to this language of sharing a small resource as we created an abundance of hospitality, refuge, and meaningful memories with family and friends. The image of abundance took root in a painting of San Pasqual.

As a wedding gift for our new home, my cousin made us a beautifully artistic handmade rendition of San Pasqual. San Pasqual is a Spanish saint considered to be the patron saint of cooks and kitchens. He was a Franciscan Friar who was known for making beautiful meals by using whatever food he had in the kitchen or garden. Out of his resources, San Pasqual could feed his friar community and any guests who would arrive.

There was always enough food for whoever was present for a meal. San Pasqual was consistently seen by his fellow friars meditating or praying when he was supposed to be cooking. Yet, meals were ready at the right moment, delicious, and plentiful. Our first home embodied much of the spirit of San Pasqual. Though our home on

138th Street was small, we always had room for family and friends—it proved to be abundant and enough.

Getting our first home was exciting and very scary. We took on a new expense and acquired a new rhythm of maintenance and upkeep. Yet, owning our home opened possibilities for hospitality and, for my husband and me, the desire to start a family. This was the perfect first home, charming, and built in 1944 with original hardwood floors and crown molding. Every area of the house was small in dimensions: three bedrooms, a 6x10 bathroom, a kitchen, a dining area, a living room, a laundry closet, and a detached garage—the whole house measured just under a thousand square feet. Though our house was not very big, we utilized every square inch of it to provide hospitality to others.

Our firstborn son was the first person we welcomed into our new home. Our home was a perfect size for the three of us as we grew into a family. We thought, *If our house is suitable for one family, it surely could be sufficient for another family to join in on the fun.* When our son was about two, we welcomed our friends to live with us for several months while they were transitioning in housing. They, too, had a young toddler plus a dog. Our friends took our second bedroom, and we turned the 10x12 office into a cozy space for the boys. Two families with two toddlers all shared one bathroom.

My favorite memories with this family were the months we lived together. As couples, we were early in our marriages, new at being parents, figuring out our lives and next steps in our journey. We shared in watching our kids, making meals, and cleaning the house. It took good communication and the ability to laugh as we shared a small space. The sharing of hearts, laughs, insight, and struggle was rich in a season of growth for us all. Soon, our friends moved out, and our home expanded in other ways.

My brother and his family lived a few hours away at the time. He had two toddlers and soon a baby was added to the mix. He and his family, my parents, and sometimes my godsister all came to our home for weekend gatherings or special occasions. Our house could hold all ten-plus of us for a long weekend. It was small, but when we all gathered together, we had fun laughing, sharing good food, and being comfortable in the small setting. As a family, we look back on those years, remembering how three kids fit in a tiny office room. Thanks to some clever bunk beds, everyone had a space to sleep. Somehow, ten-plus people were able to share one bathroom and still enjoy one another. We often giggle remembering those years in our tiny house. We can visualize a drawing of laughs and hearts surrounding our home as well as hands and feet sticking out of doors and windows. Being cramped never kept us from gathering as often as possible. Somehow, our home was always more than enough.

Eventually, we expanded our thousand-square-foot house to a two thousand-square-foot house. A new construction included expanding our kitchen and adding a second floor; this included a large open living area and an extra bathroom. The remodel was a different kind of stress and adventure. Yet, we knew our home would need more room. My husband's father and mother were actively a part of our new remodel. Each of them brought the resources of their talent, support, and encouragement as we set out on this new construction. The four of us did many things together to offset the cost of the overall remodel: cutting and placing siding, painting, framing, etc. Their contribution and celebration of this new addition were rooted in great love. Thankfully, our remodel went without a significant hitch. Yet, little did we know that the home addition would expand our family and story in new ways.

Soon after our remodel, I became pregnant with our second child—a longing that took ten years to come to fruition. There was abundant love and celebration as we welcomed our second son. The newly added room provided space for guests and an open area for our youngest to run and play in. We were fortunate to have one of our former high school students come and be our nanny for our youngest. She, too, became an additional family member. She often stopped by even when she wasn't watching our youngest to have dinner with us, watch a movie, or sometimes she would bring her niece to play with our son. Our addition expanded our home to include new family members in our daily routines and stories.

When our construction was underway, a neighbor asked, "How many rooms do you have up there?" When my husband triumphantly declared, "One large living room!" Our neighbor responded in his thick Russian accent, "One room! One room! Ahh, that's terrible!" Then he continued on his way. Yet, this one, large room served many purposes. It soon served as the perfect space for football-watching parties.

Our home became the hub to watch games during the two seasons that the Seahawks went to the Super Bowl. We had several friends and neighbors over to watch with us. It became such a habit and routine that each person who came had specific spots to sit in. In our collective, silly superstition, each person would need to sit in their assigned spots if our team was starting to lose. Football game gathering was such a pattern that our younger son often asked, "Is it Seahawks day?" Being together strengthened friendships among our neighbors and gave us a pause in our lives to eat a meal, be silly, have fun, and be in fellowship. The allotted time together strengthened bonds and created rich memories. The added big room was not terrible after all.

Our thousand-square-foot home on 138th Street expanded in many ways. Our home welcomed our two boys and many others to stay with us throughout the eighteen years we lived there. Whether the stay was for an extended time, a weekend, or a gathering, we loved having people in our home. Our home was a valuable resource of hospitality and embodied the abundant mindset of San Pasqual. Every square inch of our home created love, connection, and memories that were always more than enough.

Mi Casita para Mi Alma
(My Little Cottage for My Soul)

Who am I beyond the handprints that have touched my life?
What gifts are authentically given and created in me?
What words were inscribed into my heart, naming my essence
long before fear, protection, security, and outer voices misled my ears?

My surface self has shifted and changed.
What had defined me, given validation and purpose, have all been stripped away.
A yearning and calling from within has begun to create a commotion
unearthing a hunger and longing to know and be known entirely.

Ancient desert mothers and fathers speak of the journey within.
A "cell" or "home" found interiorly,
a place to enter with surrender and openness.
Cultivating a practice of deep listening, beholding, and paying attention.

St. Teresa of Avila calls this place an interior castle,
an inner place of learning and receiving and

a deeper understanding of extravagant love—
love that longs to create a more profound union between the
Divine and all humanity.

A sacred place is prepared just for each person, even me,
where unveiling and revealing truths occur.
Never demanding but rather a place of comfort and peace.
Extravagant love and mercy extending an ongoing invitation,
"Come within."

How do I respond to such an invitation?
This steady nudging and stirring has been occurring within me for
some time,
a voice that has become more pronounced and alluring.
Yet, I resist, pull away, hide in excuses of this all being too
abstract.

However, this voice remains steady and responds to my
hesitations.
Without a hint of accusation or fear, Love asks, "Why?"
In this gentle inquiry, Love remains assuring, without expectation
or intrusion.
Love patiently waits for my response.

Eventually, I say, "An interior castle or cell overwhelms me.
It feels demanding, filled with expectations, lonely, sterile,
uncomfortable."
As if pondering, Love simply asks,
"Could you imagine this home differently, una casita for your
soul?"

With a word, *casita*, my heart and spirit leap into creative
imagination.
A southwestern adobe home with many stories emerges from a
known place.
A tall home with a golden orange hue exterior,
with a sizable arched door that radiates "Welcome any and all."

There are many rooms throughout this home.
One is a large kitchen with long tables for many to sit. Windows are throughout, providing natural light
illuminating and giving warmth all around.

This home is nestled against a glacier mountain.
Low clouds are present in the morning and rise as the day unfolds.
Outside, there are flower beds and gardens, with a winding river nearby.
A bridge welcomes this lively setting, a bridge of favor and mercy.

As I embrace this image, I am moved to tears.
Extravagant Love sees me and smiles,
"Come, this is where your soul belongs; here is where I am with you.
Each time you cross the bridge, know all is forgotten; come as you are."

As my soul enters into this new place of love and life
I am drawn to quiet myself to listen, ponder, and pray.
The Divine and I willfully engage in knowing and being known.
With wonderful delight, saints and ancestors also meet me here.

Wounded patterns and habits present in my life are coaxed to the surface.
Each unearthing may bring a dialogue, an occasional wrestling, or even the option of fleeing.
Yet, I return knowing that with patience and accompanied by love,
healing will occur, and restoration will flourish.

Mi casita para mi alma is where I continue to meet extravagant Love.
Each time I visit, I am filled, and I am invited to share extravagant love in return.
When I cross over the bridge of tenderness, I know I am forgiven.
That extension of mercy compels me to extend grace to others.

Mi casita para mi alma is my interior home filled with love and affection.

I am welcomed each time by a chorus of voices with warm embraces saying, "You are here!"

With such love, I am learning to trust in bringing my whole self, even my enslavements.

Never shamed, but rather loved into a greater sense of significance and freedom.

Conclusion

Assembled and Stitched to Create a Whole

When I set out to create this literary quilt, I gathered several stories and poems representing various patches and fabrics of my life. Like any creative endeavor, I had to listen and notice what stories and poems wanted to come forth. It became a contemplative practice of paying attention to what was stirring in and around me. This required me to be patient, to not force the process, and to allow each piece, patch, and element of this literary quilt to emerge in its own time and utterance. In that motion, I allowed myself to be vulnerable, open, and willing to let what was deep within me come to the surface.

I discovered that the quilt of my life is beautiful. Each layer is important: base, patches, and string ties. Starting with the foundational material given to me by my family, community, and culture, this wonderful base has remained woven within who I am. It is filled with music, life, honesty, devotion, deep faith, laughter, joy, and sorrow. This material has been steady, constant, and continues to integrate with other fabric, which are the patches. These patches became a visual expression of my story.

I imagine myself stepping back to look at the overall finished work. I can't help but recognize how necessary each piece and layer are to the whole. I marvel at all the rich and splendid colors spread across this fabric canvas, including various hues representing people and experiences. Every shape and texture offer multi-dimensional components of faithful love, dedication, community, challenges, and transition, perfectly arranged corners form artistic density. All these elements highlight and inspire unique features of my life and story.

Surprisingly, in this imaginative place of stepping back and looking upon, I notice how significant the string ties are. The string ties keep the quilt together and serve as a subtle decorative accent. A curved needle pulls the string ties through the quilt as it gathers every layer in the descending and ascending movement. This same motion is also occurring within the stories of this literary quilt—rooted stories that descended into various experiences and people to then ascend into poems that give language to what was emerging. These poems are filled with lyrics, images, characters, nature, symbols, and poetic words to name the authentic aspects of myself that I am becoming. As a result, these poems, like the string ties, hold the tapestry of my life together and serve as a subtle accent of grace and love as they draw on the truth springing forward.

Thank you for joining me through my quilted memoir, on my narrative journey, and for your grace in holding the layers and components of this literary quilt. Like all artistic and reflective endeavors, there is risk in entering into the process. Identifying the elements that provide the batting, patches, and string ties to your quilt is a deeply personal and profound journey. I trust and hope that my quilt has given something of a support and encouragement for you to draw together the fabric that is uniquely you and celebrate the quilt that results.

About the Author

Adrianne Dyer was born and raised in New Mexico. She later moved to Washington state, where she lived for thirty-three years. She attended Western Washington University, where she earned her Bachelor of Arts degree in recreation with a minor in political science. She later earned her master's in pastoral studies from Seattle University, School of Theology and Ministry.

She has worked in education for twenty years in both the private and public sectors for primary and secondary education. She is a medical spiritual care provider/chaplain and spiritual companion/director. She is involved with SEEL Puget Sound; Spiritual Exercises in Everyday Life, where she serves as a spiritual companion and formation leader.

She is a Roman Catholic, who holds to the universal *catholic* expression and whose spirituality has been fashioned by Ursuline, Franciscan, Carmelite, Jesuit, and Benedictine monastic traditions.

She cultivates a mystic spirit, and her inner monk is woven into everyday life. She holds the belief that writing and listening to stories can provide an aspect of healing. Stories can embody a holistic expression as they integrate the inner and outer worlds together through experiences, metaphors, and images. Lessons and insights within a story can provide restoration and transformation.

She first published an article in ASRA Pain Medicine on "Integrating Spiritual Care in an Acute Pain Service," July 17, 2018. Later, her poems and writings have been posted on Facebook via Holy Disorder of Dancing Monk. She has had a reflection published in Abbey of the Arts: Transformative Living Through Contemplative and Expressive Arts newsletter, *Monk in the World Guest Post,* January 2024.

She is married to Kale Dyer and together they have two sons. Currently she lives overseas and serves military families who are stationed abroad. She enjoys outdoor activities, reading, writing, quilting, and spending time with family and friends.

Author Contact Information:

Email: 2023qandq@gmail.com

For more great books from Empower Press
Visit Books.GracePointPublishing.com

If you enjoyed reading *My Quilted Memoir,* and purchased it through an online retailer, please return to the site and write a review to help others find the book.